D1250934

SPECTRUM OF CATHOLIC ATTITUDES

# Spectrum of
# Catholic Attitudes

Edited by REV. ROBERT CAMPBELL, O. P.

De Paul University

*Contributors*

WILLIAM F. BUCKLEY, JR.
Editor, *National Review*

DR. DANIEL CALLAHAN
Author, *Mind of the Catholic Layman,* etc.

DR. LESLIE DEWART
Author, *The Future of Belief,* etc.

DALE FRANCIS
Publisher, *Twin Circle*

WALTER L. MATT
Publisher, *The Remnant*

DR. MARSHALL MCLUHAN
Author, *Understanding Media,* etc.

DR. FRANK J. SHEED
Author, *Theology and Sanity,* etc.

The Bruce Publishing Company/Milwaukee

# PREFACE

Following publication of *Spectrum of Protestant Beliefs*[1], which presented Protestantism from a new point of view, stressing that an individual's denomination is of much less importance than his position in the liberal-conservative spectrum, several people suggested to the editor that they would like to see a similar "spectrum analysis" of attitudes among the Catholic public. This book is the result.

Despite Vatican II and subsequent developments, many people have found it difficult to amend their life-long image of the Catholic public as a monolithic bloc. Until the furor caused by Pope Paul VI's encyclical on birth control, few seemed to realize the radical nature of the split in Catholic ranks, both among clergy and laity. The purpose of this book is to "tell it as it is," by graphically presenting the increasing divergence of beliefs and attitudes among Catholics today.

Laymen were chosen as contributors because most readers will feel, rightly or wrongly, that laymen are freer to express their true opinions than are clerics. Each of the contributors voices the attitudes prevailing in his own segment of the spectrum. Each is influential in further shaping opinions in his milieu. The reader

[1] The Bruce Publishing Company, Milwaukee, 1968. William Hamilton, co-author with Thomas Altizer of *Radical Theology and the Death of God*, is spokesman for the radical element in Protestantism on a variety of topics; Bishop James A. Pike, author and theologian-in-residence at the Center for the Study of Democratic Institutions, represents liberals; John Warwick Montgomery, author and chairman of the division of church history at Trinity Divinity School, speaks for the confessional groups; Carl F. H. Henry, then editor of *Christianity Today*, presents new evangelical views; and Dr. Bob Jones, president of Bob Jones University, represents the fundamentalists.

will quickly decide with which spokesman he most closely identifies.

No attempt has been made to divide the Catholic spectrum into named segments as was done with the Protestant spectrum. This decision was made because the divergence of opinions among Catholics is not as yet as focused or publicized as that among Protestants. Moreover, any names given the bands of the Catholic spectrum would be loaded with pejorative connotations, making it unfair to give any segment a name which its members would generally reject.[2] The terms "ultra-liberal," "moderate," and "ultra-conservative" immediately load the dice in favor of the man in the middle, assigning him the role of calm reason and casting the ultras as wild-eyed fanatics. But is the true situation *"in medio stat virtus"* or "I would you were hot or cold, but because you are lukewarm I vomit you out of my mouth"?

The title, *Spectrum of Catholic Attitudes*, does not imply that all the opinions in this book are Catholic in the sense of being in harmony with the teachings of Popes and Councils. One of the contributors candidly describes his views as "undoubtedly heretical on a number of issues of fundamental theological significance." The attitudes expressed in this book are Catholic at least in the sense that they have currency among some Catholics.

How widely are these views held by Catholics today? Appendix A has assembled some data from recent surveys that will help the reader see the relative number of Catholics who agree or disagree with each of our contributors.

[2] The contributors to *Spectrum of Protestant Beliefs* were quite willing to accept the names "fundamentalist," "new evangelical," "radical," etc. Indeed most of them already thought of themselves in those terms.

# CONTENTS

# PRESENTING THE CONTRIBUTORS

## WILLIAM F. BUCKLEY, JR.

Considering our contributors in alphabetical order gets us off
to a colorful start. *Time* reports that William F. Buckley, Jr.,
"leading U.S. ideologue of the right and celebrated for his wit . . .
is everywhere in evidence these days." His TV clawings with Gore
Vidal gave a dash of color to a dull Republican National Convention in Miami. After Buckley had scored some points in the clash
he turned to Vidal and asked "What do you have to say to that?"
Vidal: "I must admit I wasn't listening." Buckley: "That is your
trouble, Gore, for years now you haven't been listening." Indeed everywhere in evidence, Mr. Buckley has just written an
article for *Esquire* on Truman Capote's masked ball (the only conservative invited?) and taught at the leftist New School for Social
Research, an employment as improbable as being keynoter for the
Democratic National Convention.

William Buckley is editor of the conservative *National Review*
(circulation 110,000) whose $200,000 loss (sued by Linus Paul-
ing—Buck Oley won) in lawyer's fees he takes blithely in stride.
He writes a column "On the Right" which appears three times a
week and is syndicated in over 250 newspapers. Further facts:
age 42, sixth of ten children in a family that played touch football,
"but not as ferociously as the Kennedys." He has a lovely wife,
Patricia, and one child Christopher, age 15, is the author of *God
and Man at Yale, The Unmaking of a Mayor* and several other
books. He is much in demand as a lecturer despite his $1000 fee,
is an ardent yachtsman, and was soundly trounced by Lindsay in

the race for mayor of New York. When I mentioned to him that some of my acquaintances in New York had voted for him, Mr. Buckley shot back "I hope they have confessed it," flashing his brilliant smile. The demands of polemics do not permit him to be as completely charming on his weekly TV show "Firing Line" as he is in private.

Although he is Mr. Conservative in his political and social approach, Buckley feels that "temperamentally I am not of the conservative breed." His dash and style do not square with the usual conservative image. Parked in the hallway of his home is a Honda. Frequently he dismisses his chauffeur and zips through clogged New York traffic on the Honda, leaving a trail of excited "Wasn't that . . . ?" His is hardly the "always griping and clipping coupons" image attributed to conservatives. For a parallel one has to look to the late South African poet, Roy Campbell, fighter for Franco, who delighted in dangling his wife by her ankles from a 20th story window. (More remarkably, she is reported to have enjoyed it.)

In this book Mr. Buckley offers some surprises to those who have envisioned him as totally on the right. He opts for birth control, for giving priests the right to marry, for divorce. Thus in religion his liberal temperament triumphs at least partially over his conservative philosophy. "The *Triumph* crowd considers me heterodox," he admits.

Mr. Buckley's contributions to this book were given extemporaneously and tape recorded.

## DANIEL CALLAHAN

*Commonweal* has been called the most influential force in shaping the opinions of avant garde Catholics in America. A former executive editor of that journal and a prolific writer (*Mind of the Catholic Layman, Honesty in the Church, The New Church*), Dr. Callahan has had some claim to being the person whose ideas are most likely to gain currency in liberal Catholic circles. However he disclaims this role: "I don't consciously think of myself as a 'shaper of public opinion' at all;

that is something I prefer to leave to the preachers and prophets, and I consider myself neither . . . My training was in
philosophy and I see myself as exercising one of the philosopher's
roles: probing and attempting to clarify . . . While I suppose some
might see my recent writings as 'radical' or excessively liberal, I
don't. Indeed, I have been more critical of liberals lately than of
conservatives; but the stance of my criticism is not usually a conservative stance—it's some other stance, my own."

Dr. Callahan is a graduate of Yale University (one thing he has
in common with his opposing ideologue, William F. Buckley, Jr.)
and received his Ph.D. in philosophy from Harvard. Dr. Callahan
is married to Sydney Cornelia Callahan ("she is a significant help
to me in my work"), who is also a writer—*The Illusion of Eve* and
the much discussed *Beyond Birth Control,* urging the acceptance
of birth control and admission of women to the priesthood. The
Callahans have six children.

Dr. Callahan has the distinction of having taught at more
Protestant schools than any other Catholic scholar: he was the
first Catholic to be appointed to the Religion faculty at Brown
University, he has taught at Union Theological Seminary in New
York City, at the Graduate Theological Union in Berkeley, and at
Temple University. He has contributed to numerous scholarly
publications and has edited several books, among them *Federal
Aid and Catholic Schools* (1964) and *The Secular City Debate*
(1966). At present Dr. Callahan is writing a book on abortion
with the help of grants from the Population Council and the Ford
Foundation.

Concerning the modern Catholic Church, Dr. Callahan is
quoted in *Overview* as saying: "Out of an eagerness to avoid all
dichotomies and any semblance of a monolith, the most unlikely
bed-mates are welcomed into the household. A Roman Catholic
can be just about anything he pleases these days, at least if he is
an academic or a layman. He can be a Jew, a Protestant, a Marxist,
an empiricist, an idealist, whatever he likes; it may take some
doing to pull it off, but he can usually manage it by invoking—
well, say, by invoking the later figure of Jacques Maritain as
a horrid example of what happens when people or the Church

think they once and for all have got hold of The Truth. I am an empiricist myself, can't stand Teilhard, and haven't the faintest notion of what some of my colleagues are talking about when they speak with hushed voice about 'the transcendent.' But they tolerate me and I tolerate them; we pat ourselves on the back for our new openness. It's just as cozy as the old crib ever was, and maybe equally inconsequential . . . Someone is going to have to figure out how to put the pieces together again."

## LESLIE DEWART

Dr. Dewart's book *The Future of Belief* has been enthusiastically praised by both the Catholic and the Protestant intellectual community—and also controverted. "This book has a chance of being a turning point in Roman Catholic thought" is the judgment of Gerard Gloyan, Catholic theologian. Harvey Cox of "Secular City" fame says: "Dewart is in many ways *more* radical than the death of God theologians. His is a theism that includes atheism, the only possible theism for today." And Bishop James A. Pike hails Dewart as "a soul mate. The man of the Roman communion who most closely expresses my own ideas." *The Ecumenist* magazine devoted a full issue to four reviews of his book, a sign of recognition to delight the heart of any author. In his book Dewart urges a de-Hellenization of Christian doctrine and its thorough re-interpretation in the light of modern thought and developments. As Dr. Dewart says "The central question treated in my book is 'can Christian belief evolve despite the fact that it is supernatural and revealed?' " He is following this book with *The Foundations of Belief*, to appear in the spring of 1969, which will deal with the more basic question "Can Christian belief evolve despite the fact that it is true and its object is real?"

Dr. Dewart, born in Spain in 1922 (Gonzalez y Duarte), was a bomber-reconnaisance pilot with the Royal Canadian Air Force during World War II, is the father of four children, and is now Professor of Religious Studies at St. Michael's College, University of Toronto. (A fellow faculty member with Marshall McLuhan.)

He is associate editor of *Continuum* and of *Internationale Dialog-zeitschrift.*

In addition to *The Future of Belief* he is the author of *Christianity and Revolution* (1963) and more than one hundred articles for magazines and journals. This is his eighth symposium.

## DALE FRANCIS

Dale Francis considers himself a newspaperman. He has worked as everything from police reporter to daily columnist, sports writer to editor, on daily newspapers in Ohio. As a local preacher in the Methodist Church, he was pastor of a church in a predominantly Catholic area of Ohio for four years. He became a Catholic in 1945 while serving in the U.S. Air Force. Since that time, his major field has been Catholic journalism.

He was the founding editor of diocesan newspapers in North Carolina and Texas; he founded the University of Notre Dame Press and served as director of publications; for two years he was the director of the Bureau of Information of what was then known as the National Catholic Welfare Conference; for five years he headed a Catholic information center in North Carolina and conducted a telephone talk show on religion over the most powerful station in the state; for two years he served as director of the Defense of the Faith for the diocese of Mantanzas in Cuba and wrote a column for the Havana Post; he taught theology at St. Edward's University; was a columnist and executive editor for *Our Sunday Visitor;* is now publisher and columnist for a new Catholic weekly, *Twin Circle;* founded *Operation Understanding,* the first Catholic weekly designed to carry on a dialogue with Protestant clergymen, for which he won the Catholic Press Association's St. Francis de Sales award; founded *Voices of Our Brothers,* a twice monthly newsletter in which he summarizes significant articles from a hundred Protestant and Catholic publications. He has written two books, numerous articles, short stories and poetry for more than 50 religious and secular magazines.

Of his public role in the Catholic Church Mr. Francis says:

"I envision my role in the Catholic press as one in which I hope

to stay ahead of movements. In 1946, as editor of the North Carolina Catholic, I editorialized strongly for the rights of Negroes
and later in Texas a major editorial campaign was for open
housing.

"I spoke in dozens of cities during the mid-40's, urging that
Catholics recognize they fulfilled the meaning of being Catholics
by their action among men, telling them they saw Christ best
when they saw Him in the least of their fellow-men.

"I started my ecumenical work among Protestants in the early
50's, and Operation Understanding, the first weekly effort to bring
Catholics and Protestants into dialogue started in 1957.

"Through my writing I've tried to introduce the public to new
movements in the Church—Citizens for Educational Freedom and
the Cursillos are two such movements that gained their first
national attention through my writings.

"Today I am concerned for fidelity to the traditional theological
truths in the Catholic Church and an acceptance by Catholics of
the Magisterium of the Church. This, I believe, is the critical issue
ahead of us. I am appalled by the repetition of mistakes by some
of today's Catholic theologians that were made in Protestantism
more than half a century ago. Much of this theology is not recog-
nizably Catholic. Vatican II was a good and necessary step in
renewal but much of what is being proposed today has no relationship to what was decided at Vatican II. The total disregard for
the Magisterium of the Church, the castigation of the Pope whenever he speaks, are not, I think, leading to schism but they are
already schismatic.

"In all of that is happening, I have a great confidence in the
ordinary people. As Arianism was finally defeated by the faithful
when theologians and even some bishops succumbed to it, so do
I believe that those who today deny traditional Catholic doctrine,
who whittle the meaning out of such beliefs as that of the Real
Presence in the Eucharist, the Virgin Birth, the meaning of the
Incarnation, will be overcome by a people still loyal to the traditional teachings of the Church.

"So the meaning of my allegiance to the traditional teachings of
the Church will not be misunderstood, I am not a Traditionalist.

Twenty years ago I wrote for *Amen,* the publication of the Vernacular Society. I am for renewal, only opposed to what I see as destruction."

## WALTER L. MATT

*The Wanderer* (circulation 30,000), published fortnightly in St. Paul, has long been considered the most bed-rock conservative Catholic newspaper in America. Its basic policy is that "without absolute loyalty to the bishops and Pope there is no Catholicism." It denounced Hitler and the Nazi movement long before they came to power and had the honor of being among the very first publications banned in Germany as soon as Dr. Goebbels became Minister of Propaganda. The paper has been equally vigorous in attacking Communism. Of this "severe, old-fashioned, aggressively Catholic, best loved, best hated" publication Walter L. Matt was associate editor and later editor from 1945 until 1967, when he left the *Wanderer* to found *The Remnant,* a fortnightly newsletter. He describes the purpose of his new venture as "an attempt, however modest and circumscribed, to draw recruits to the cause of Christ and His Church and, whilst avoiding contentious factionalism, rally what is left of the truly devoted 'people of God' —or loyal remnant of little people—to stand firm on the side of Christ and His Holy Church, and, with God's help, strive by all means but principally by living the full Christian life of penance and prayer and total commitment to Jesus through Mary, to help turn back the tide of an all-engulfing materialism, secularism and practical atheism which have nearly succeeded even now in eliminating the last vestiges of what was once Christendom from the face of the earth."

Walter L. Matt, "slender, shy, serious-minded," is a graduate of St. Thomas College. He was awarded the Bronze Star for his work with Army Public Relations and Intelligence Service during World War II. He is the father of seven pre-teenage children. Mr. Matt has written and lectured for many years on the papal program of individual and social reform and is the author of a number of pamphlets and brochures.

## MARSHALL MCLUHAN

A *Newsweek* Special Report on Marshall McLuhan says: "The Oracle of Toronto thinks big—his theory of communications offers nothing less than an explanation of all human culture, past, present and future . . . McLuhan's teaching is radical, new, animated by high intelligence, and capable of moving people to social action . . . He can only be considered a stimulating thinker on a scale quite similar to Freud and Einstein." Quite a tribute for a professor of English at St. Michael's College, University of Toronto.

The two books which launched Marshall McLuhan into his present orbit of lectures at fantastic fees, best-selling books, and public acclaim were *The Gutenberg Galaxy* (1962) and *Understanding Media* (1964). His theory that a society's means of communication largely determines every other aspect of that society ("the medium is the message") has won an impressive reception. General Electric, IBM, Bell Telephone, Container Corporation and the publishers of America's largest magazines have had him address their top executives. When he gave me a gracious interview in his home he and his attractive wife had just that hour returned from a week in San Juan where he had been addressing a group called, if I remember correctly, the Young Presidents, men who were presidents of corporations before reaching the age of forty. A prominent advertising man says of McLuhan, "he is an Archimedes who has given the ad industry levers to move the world." Praise that is more likely to bring a shudder than a glow to this latter day Archimedes.

Marshall McLuhan was born in Edmonton, Alberta, in 1911. After taking his M.A. at the University of Manitoba in 1934 he went to Cambridge for two years and returned to begin his teaching career at the University of Wisconsin. He became a Catholic in 1937, has six children ("all my daughters are beautiful," which impartial observers confirm) and in 1967-68 held the Albert Schweitzer Chair in the Humanities at Fordham University, a post which paid $100,000 a year for salary and research expenses.

His latest works are *Counterblast* (1968), *War and Peace in the Global Village* (1968), and *Through the Vanishing Point: Space in Poetry and Painting* (1968).

When I inquired as to his concept of his role as a shaper of public opinion he answered with one word: "probe." In a recent book he enlarged on this: "Most of my work in the media is like that of a safecracker. In the beginning I don't know what's inside. I just set myself down in front of the problem and begin to work. I grope, I probe, I listen, I test—until the tumblers fall and I'm in."

His prose is not noted for its lucidity. He says "Clear prose indicates the absence of thought." People who have difficulty understanding his writing may derive comfort from the remark attributed to him: "I don't understand everything I write, after all, my stuff is very difficult." And those who disagree with what they understand of his theories can derive similar comfort: "I don't necessarily agree with everything I say."

Just-born is the Marshall McLuhan Newsletter, put out by the Human Development Corporation of New York City. "This entirely different kind of Newsletter will be a startling, shocking, monthly early warning system for our era of instant change."

## F. J. SHEED

Frank J. Sheed has probably the best claim to the title of "grand old man of Catholic letters." An Australian, graduate of Sydney University, F. J. Sheed and his wife Maisie Ward founded the London publishing house of Sheed and Ward in 1926, and its American counterpart in 1933. Among the great names they made familiar to the English-speaking public were Jacques Maritain, Paul Claudel, Leon Bloy, Karl Adam, Romano Guardini and Ronald Knox of a past generation, followed by Hans Küng, Edward Schillebeeckx, and Karl Rahner in our own time. Mr. Sheed's own numerous writings include the highly acclaimed *Theology and Sanity, Theology for Beginners,* and *To Know Christ Jesus.* Soon to appear is a collection of his recent newspaper columns entitled *Is It The Same Church?* His is presently preparing a book *Theology and Sanity for Grown-Ups* which studies the impact of philosophy and Scripture research on theology.

John Courtney Murray paid this high tribute to Frank Sheed's contribution to theology: "He has labored as a layman, for laymen, in behalf of a theology of the laity and for the laity. The edifice of theological thought that he has erected, in book after book and in innumerable lectures, is at once a monument and a foundation. In lands of the English language his name leads all the rest, on a list that fortunately is not finished. History will accord him honor."

In addition to his writing, lecturing and publishing activities, Frank Sheed has been a speaker for the Catholic Evidence Guild for over forty years, explaining the Catholic religion on street corners in such places as Times Square in New York and Hyde Park in London. Of his theological stance someone said "He has more sympathy with the liberals than have most conservatives, more sympathy with the conservatives than have most liberals. He has the rare quality of extending his ecumenism to include fellow-Catholics with whom he does not agree."

Mr. Sheed is one of the very few laymen to be awarded a doctorate of Sacred Theology, *honoris causa,* by the Sacred Congregation of Seminaries and Universities in Rome (1955).

# INTRODUCTION

"I look at the priests in this house and I say to myself 'I don't know you. I have nothing in common with you.' This bunch of antediluvian characters hasn't had a fresh thought since they were ordained. Why, I have much more in common with some of my atheist and agnostic friends than I have with these Neanderthal types." The priest speaking was not a youngster—in a year or two he would have the traumatic experience of reaching his fortieth birthday. His voice vibrated with emotion as he proclaimed his alienation from a dozen fellow priests of the same religious community. Ostensibly these men have similar outlooks on life— all are Catholics, all are priests, all are members of the same religious order, all are living in the same house. In reality they are worlds apart. Superficially they are brothers, in basic ideology they are mortal enemies. By keeping their relationships on a superficial level they are able to be civil to one another.

His sentiments were seconded by his companion, a graying priest in his fifties, regarded by some as "the kindliest priest in our community" and by others as a "gentle Heinrich of the left." "I have the warmest feelings for those outside the Church, whether they are Protestants, Jews, Buddhists, atheists, Communists, or whatever, but for some of the priests in this community," he gritted, "and for the s.o.b.'s in the Curia, for all the reactionaries in the Church, I just can't summon up any feelings of Christian charity."

The youngest priest in the group, in his mid-thirties, concurred. "I have stopped buying Schick razor blades since I learned that Schick contributes money to the *Wanderer* Forum." His voice rang with righteous conviction. "Have you noticed the quarter-page ad that Schick has in almost every issue of the *Wanderer?*" This priest prided himself on his tolerance and breadth of viewpoint. Had someone suggested that he stop buying a product because the manufacturer supported Communist projects he would have been revolted by the narrowness of the suggestion.

This scene, with variations, is repeated thousands of times every day throughout the world as liberal Catholics voice their dissatisfaction with their conservative brethren and with the "institutionalized Church." The image of the Catholic public as a monolithic bloc has been shattered even for the man in the street by the tide of dissent evoked by Pope Paul's Creed and even more vigorously by his encyclical on birth control. (Though some still cling sufficiently to the monolith image as to be apprehensive of a flood of Catholic babies resulting from the Pope's rejection of birth control.)

The present "most serious outburst of dissent the Catholic Church has experienced in centuries" (*Time*) is the flood tide of a current of liberalism which has always flowed underground in Catholicism, surfacing at points in history (Erasmus and renaissance humanism, the modernist crisis of the early 1900's, etc.) and recently brought to crest by technological developments, the world-wide cry for liberation from restrictions, and more particularly by Vatican II and the resulting increased freedom of expression.

Although the crisis has come into sharpest focus in the birth control controversy, most commentators have realized that the issues run much deeper. Catholics are faced with a crisis of authority: whom shall I believe, the Pope and the theologians who support him or those theologians who say that traditional Catholic beliefs are no longer binding? Is the faith unchanging in its essentials, as the Pope's Creed would indicate, or is it evolving? Is the Pope the supreme authority in matters religious, or does authority lie ultimately with the flock, the People of God? Will the real Catholic Church please stand up? Does freedom of conscience mean I am morally free to disagree with a defined teaching of the Church? Which is most important, achieving human fulfillment in this life or attaining eternal salvation? Or should I shunt both these considerations into the background in favor of working to make this a better world?

The opposing factions in Catholicism seem to be crystallizing into two classical attitudes, just as occurred long ago in Protestantism. On the right are those who emphasize the supremacy of God, the unchanging character of the truths He has revealed, man's duty of obedience to God, and the importance of eternal salvation—"what does it profit a man if he gain the whole world and lose his own soul." On the left are those who emphasize man's freedom and dignity, who hold that truth is an evolving thing, even to the point of scrapping teachings previously held to be most sacred, who proclaim the importance of individual fulfillment here and now, and the building of a more humane society for the future. Of the "two great commandments," love God above all and love your neighbor as yourself, those on the right more frequently appeal to the first and those on the left more frequently appeal to the second. Of the dwindling conservative minority William F. Buckley, Jr. says "they speak in whispers and walk about furtively."

One of the most significant human events in our generation has been the shift in popular Catholic attitudes from the first of these outlooks, what we might call the "supernatural" outlook, to the second, or "natural" outlook. In a poll conducted in 1966 by Dr. Gallup's Public Opinion Survey for the *Catholic Digest* the question was asked: "Which do you think is more important for the church to do—to convert people to a spiritual belief so that they can earn a happy life after death; or to teach people how to live better every day with all other people?" Thirty-five per cent of Catholics responded "both," 55% favored the "living better with others," and a small nine per cent placed the emphasis on salvation. Fourteen years ago when the same poll was taken almost twice that per cent of Catholics gave first importance to the "happy life after death."

Catholics over forty can verify in their own experience this shift in attitudes. As recently as the end of World War II the prevailing mind-set among priests and laity was one of orthodoxy.

"Purity of doctrine" was the watchword. A Catholic felt ashamed even privately to disagree with traditional Catholic views, and those who expressed disagreement were regarded as "kooks," disloyal and dangerous. The standard which determined the excellence of any theological opinion was, "is it faithful to the magisterium." The term "liberal" was an epithet which could provoke a fight. To be accused of being a liberal was tantamount to a charge of "pinko." Frequently brandished was Leo XIII's dictum—still featured on the masthead of the *Wanderer*—that no one can be both a liberal and a Catholic.

Today the mind-set of the average priest or layman is almost completely reversed. Orthodoxy as the prevailing standard of excellence has been replaced by the concepts of aggiornamento, ecumenism, and secularity, all focusing on change. In any controversy the status quo proponents are guilty unless proven innocent and the change proponents are ipso facto courageous crusaders.

The former "doctrinally sound" stance favored by priests has been replaced by a "liberaler-than-thou" competition. "You use the Dutch canon? I prefer the Hippolytus canon. It's much simpler." Or "you should have seen my students eat it up when I demythologized papal infallibility today!" Or "you still say the breviary? How square can you get!" In the mind-set of twenty years ago a priest who stated that he did not believe in angels would have been regarded as a very strange bird indeed by his colleagues. Even private expression of such a view might have resulted in a reprimand from his bishop. Today's mind-set expresses itself: "You still believe in angels? I thought everyone had given up that medieval nonsense."

In this "liberaler-than-thou" gamesmanship the most devastating ploy is to tag your opponent a conservative. Of course ultraconservative, or by extension, Birchite, is even worse. The hapless victim cringes under the verbal lash. Once "labeled with this libel" his credibility is ruined in many circles and his contract as a teacher is in danger of non-renewal for "failure to maintain professional standards." Formerly the crushing riposte was "why that's heretical!" Now the coup de grace is administered by "that is a beautiful piece of Tridentine theology." The victim slinks away. Or he may be goaded into a wildly outré burst of ultra-liberalism in a frenetic effort to restore his image.

According to "death-of-God" proponent, Thomas J. J. Altizer, all the attacks on his "Christian atheism" views have come from Protestants. He states that he outdoes himself with shocking statements in a futile attempt to evoke protests from Catholic theologians. And small wonder. The Catholic theologian who would dare attack the death-of-God people would find himself buried in a blizzard of letters to the editor: "unecumenical, traditional, uninformed, narrow-minded, conservative, insensitive." Any one of these epithets is enough to send him reeling back in horror at the credibility gap opening to engulf him. Once he is branded as a conservative who will invite him to lecture, who will solicit his contribution to a symposium, who will publish his books and articles, who will recommend him for full professor?

The one-up-manship endemic to human relations has become one-left-manship among Catholic priests and lay intellectuals. The players jockey for positions on the left. You win five points by sneering at the curia, a modest little victory easily within the grasp of the mere beginner. Admission that you no longer say the rosary was once good for five points but now most groups actually penalize the player who is so quaint as to use this outmoded gambit. Endorsement of birth control is shopworn but before *Humanae Vitae* was still good for ten points if done with skill and wit; since the encyclical the premium has shot up to 25 points. "Pardon me, I must take my Pill" by a Catholic matron is now good for 25 to 50 points, depending on whether she gives the impression she is joking or serious.

Scoffing at the existence of angels—15 points. Denying the "physical interpretation of the Virgin Birth" is good for 25 points with cognoscenti but may only glaze the eyes of your average competitor. Rejecting the transcendency of God is also an erratic ploy—with a knowledgeable group it scores a 50 point coup, but in most circles it will merely be a wasted turn. The point value of all these gambits is increased tenfold if embodied in a published article, twenty-fold if in a book. Leaving the Church ordinarily wins the game, topped only by the de luxe pay-off for leaving the Church and writing a book denouncing its corruption. Here we have the folk-hero who has replaced the ascetic saint as an object for veneration if not always imitation by the Catholic public.

A virtuoso performance seldom matched in my limited experience was given by an unmarried college girl. In the presence of myself and two of her sorority sisters she remarked with wry amusement "my parents really raised hell when they found my birth control pills." Heady with this 100 point coup she soon found opportunity to describe the part of the sexual act she most enjoyed. Tasteless overkill. One of her sorority sisters made a feeble attempt to remain in competition and was reduced to groveling defeat with "but you are still in the Church. You are a hypocrite. I left the Church when I was seventeen."

*Views of the contributors to this book*

A few vignettes to whet the reader's appetite:

*God*

"With Jesus Christ I had a very early love affair." (Buckley)
"Once upon a time I did believe in the Trinity." (Callahan)
"I found crowds fascinated by the doctrine of the Trinity, finding light and nourishment in it as in no other." (Sheed)

*Bible*

"I just don't see how, with the intelligence that God granted us, we can believe that the Bible did not err." (Buckley)

*Infallibility of the Pope*

"Hardly anyone in the Church really believes in the infallibility of the Pope." (Callahan)
"If there be no voice to say 'That is wrong,' or 'This is true,' then we have no way of knowing what Christ wanted us to know." (Sheed)

*Eucharist*

"If the Eucharist is only a symbol, to hell with it." (Francis)

*Hell*

"The traditional idea of hell is infantile." (Dewart)

"The mood of the moment is to flick Satan aside. He was not so dismissed by Christ." (Sheed)

*Freedom of conscience*

"Somebody, hell, everybody, has remarked that probably more damage has been done in the world by people who intend to do good than by people who intend to commit evil." (Buckley)

*Catholic schools*

"Our Catholic schools are perhaps doomed not only to fail of their purpose but become instead agents of destruction." (Matt)

"As the world environment becomes increasingly programmed into a universal teaching machine, Catholic schools as places to acquire instruction suited to use in the outer world would become quite useless." (McLuhan)

*Social issues*

"It is not an obvious violation of the marital ideal to permit contraception." (Buckley)

"It is important to remove sexual 'sins,' other than the obviously exploitative kind, from the category of important transgressions." (Callahan)

"The non-white races realize that 'integration' is a false and illusory kind of goal." (McLuhan)

"We should repudiate rather than explain away those passages in Scripture which have provided an apparent warrant for anti-Semitism." (Callahan)

*Trends in the Church*

"Liturgical experts are more likely than not to be out of touch with the mind and heart of the rest of us." (Sheed)

"The trend is toward socialization and democratization of the Church. Christianity in the future may become a do-it-yourself affair." (Dewart)

"Left-wing Catholicism is building new, up-to-date theological dream houses; most of them seem to me flimsy and highly flammable." (Callahan)

## New Orientation Among the Churches

The picture that emerges from a full reading of the contributions to this book is the complete alienation of the men on the left from those on the right. On what do Daniel Callahan and Walter Matt agree? Both consider themselves Roman Catholics, but there the similarity ends. Even on such a bed-rock fundamental as the concept of God their ideas are contradictory. Matt holds to the concept of God as Catholic teaching has always presented it, while Callahan says "It is not that God (of the Christian tradition) is dead; he never was in the first place." Point by point comparison of their views on the 28 other topics reveals basic disagreement on all—except that both condemn anti-Semitism. But even here their ideas of causes and cures would run completely counter to each other. Interestingly enough, an opposition to anti-Semitism is the only point on which all seven contributors are unanimous, though of course with variations in their approach. The same was true of the *Spectrum of Protestant Beliefs*: the five contributors agreed on only one point, opposition to anti-Semitism.

Comparison of the "left" in this book with the "left" in the Protestant spectrum reveals another fact which will come as no surprise to those who have been following religious developments. That is the almost complete identification of the Catholic left and the Protestant left on gut issues. The liberals of all churches find each other "amazingly enlightened and similar in outlook." Leslie Dewart and Daniel Callahan would find great fellowship with William Hamilton and Bishop Pike. At a cocktail party they would have a jolly good time denouncing U.S. policy in Vietnam, comparing notes on the inadequacies of traditional beliefs and structures, or possibly laying plans for a joint civil rights demonstration. It is quite likely that the four of them have had exactly this fellowship at a cocktail party somewhere sometime. Of Catholic Leslie Dewart, Protestant Bishop Pike says "he is a soul mate . . . the man in the Roman communion who most closely expresses my own ideas." Protestant radical theologian William Hamilton says of Catholic radical Eugene Fontinell and Jewish radical Rabbi Richard Rubenstein (*After Auschwitz*): "One of the most interesting theological experiences I've had was an all night teach-in that I shared with Richard Rubenstein of Pittsburgh and Eugene Fontinell of Queen's College at the University of Rochester in 1966. Here, without compromising the radical differences among us, one saw three men working very close to the same position, each in his own way, and all of them quite clear that they were faithful members of their own tradition."

The message of the *Spectrum of Protestant Beliefs* is that denominations are "out," ideological orientation is "in." In Protestantism, a person's denominational affiliation is no longer a reliable indication of his stance on religious, moral or social questions. A liberal Baptist (Harvey Cox) has no fellowship with a conservative Baptist (Billy Graham); they agree on nothing except that the Pope is not infallible. A liberal Lutheran has no fellowship with a conservative Lutheran: ask Martin E. Marty and John Warwick Montgomery, both Missouri Synod Lutherans, what they think of each other. But a liberal Baptist and a liberal Lutheran find great empathy in each other's views, and the conservative Baptist and conservative Lutheran would accept each other as "born-again children of God." On religious and moral and social issues a re-alignment of forces has taken place, no longer on denominational lines but along ideological lines.

Now the same situation is emerging in Protestant-Catholic relations. The new alignments are not Protestant vs. Catholic but Protestant and Catholic liberals vs. Protestant and Catholic conservatives. Recently Billy Graham acknowledged the "tremendous cooperation" the Catholic Church has given to his crusades and added "I am much closer to Catholic theology (traditional) than I am to the extreme liberal theology of some Protestants." On the liberal side, Dutch Bishop Jan Willebrands is reported to have said after the Pope issued his Creed: "At some moments I feel myself nearer to Christian brothers in other churches than to some brothers in my own church with whom I live in communion."

Will this de facto situation be formalized by a break between Catholic liberals and the conservative Catholic minority, followed by an institutional union between Catholic and Protestant liberals, perhaps along the lines of the Council on Church Unity, a proposed merger between ten Protestant denominations? Not likely. Unless, of course, Rome begins to show its teeth. At present the liberals are not all that eager to form one superchurch. Most seem content to continue with the present unity of ideals, goals, and political and social action.

Will there be any formalized alignment of the Catholic right with the Protestant right? Much less likely. Prickly with principles, any rapprochement between these groups poses the same problems as two porcupines making love. Sooner or later someone gets stuck and doesn't want to play any more. This is the perennial problem perilling cooperation between conservatives of any stripe, in any project. Billy Graham's expressed sympathy for traditional Catholic theology was considerably chilled by Pope Paul's encyclical on birth control. To date there has been no ecumenism between Catholic right and Protestant right. Though both groups agree on basic Christian revelation—the transcendence of God, the Trinity, Divinity of Christ, Virgin Birth, Resurrection, Ascension—the Catholic right is as emphatic in its proclamation of papal infallibility and devotion to Mary as the Protestant right is in rejecting these doctrines. Leading fundamentalist Bob Jones is as devoted as the Pope to the Apostle's Creed but denounces the Catholic Church as the "whore of Babylon."

# MARSHALL McLUHAN ON PRIVATE OPINIONS ON CHURCH DOCTRINE

One of the contradictions inherent in Vatican II and therefore in current Catholic awareness is the tendency to accept private points of view in verbal and doctrinal matters while stressing corporate participation and involvement in all liturgical concerns. Is this not a simple reversal of the 16th century situation of the Catholic Church? At that time the efforts of the Church to centralize itself bureaucratically with the aid of the new print technology resulted in the utmost stress on uniform doctrinal positions and a relaxation of the means of corporate involvement in liturgical action. For a Catholic to be asked his private point of view on the first fourteen topics in the "spectrum" offered here seems to me meaningless. It results from the same technological changes that compel political candidates to abandon policies and goals and instead to stress their IMAGE. The reversal by which a Catholic is now supposed to develop a personal position on mysteries and doctrines that are themselves the prime means of corporate participation could only result from the belated extension of literacy to the Catholic world. The Protestant communities of the Reformation enjoyed the benefits of private views of all corporate mysteries and depended primarily on hymn singing as a non-literate form of depth participation for corporate worship. These Protestant hymns have now been added to the Catholic liturgy with emotional effects that are as bizarre as are the intellectual effects of private opinions about corporate doctrine.

Charity is not a point of view. How any point of view whatever could be a means of participation in the Mystical Body is something which only the newly literate Catholic laity can answer or explain. May it not be somewhat like the conflicting effects of electric technology when it impinges upon semi-literate or non-literate societies? Electric technology is tribal, inclusive and involving. It is this instant and organic technology that fosters the new liturgical and ecumenical unity. The old technology of alphabetic literacy always and everywhere created the exactly opposite result. Now that latter-day literacy has impinged upon the formerly tribal Catholic laity, the result seems to be a quaint and exotic Protestantism under Catholic auspices.

In the 16th century when the book was new, public liturgy was fragmented. Many of the Catholic clergy felt compelled by the new hardware environment of the book to embark upon a private and inner and non-sacramental and non-liturgical worship. Exactly the same hardware created a huge centralism of bureaucracy in politics and in commerce and in religion. Rome centralized and bureaucratized; the Pope became an earthly monarch. Kings and princes became the heads of the Protestant churches.

Today with electric software or information, all these tendencies reverse. Rome ceases to be central and bureaucratic. The Pope ceases to be an earthly potentate. The liturgy which had been fragmented before is recreated in a new unity. Whereas some of the clergy had mistaken the printed book for the inner life of the spirit, many of the Catholic clergy now mistake the new software environment for the mystical body. They feel compelled to abandon a bureaucratic Rome for a miasmatic involvement in mankind at large.

The Gutenberg revolution was visual hardware. The electric revolution is acoustic. Hardware congealed and legalized Catholic doctrine. Software blurs it into a kind of echo chamber of all religions at once.

The voice of the Pope has nothing to do with any technology, anymore than the Church does. The Incarnation was the ultimate extension of man, the ultimate technology. Electricity is for the birds.

SPECTRUM OF CATHOLIC ATTITUDES

# 1. THE CONCEPT OF GOD

## I. BUCKLEY

My concept of God is anthropomorphic in the sense that I can and do visualize Jesus Christ and believe Him to have been divine. But I don't have any residual notions of God the Father as being shaped as a human being. I do think of God as an entity and as being intelligent and concerned and invocable. That would be my definition.

I am only dimly aware of some of the trends in theology a) because I am not a theologian, b) because I choose not to be a theologian. If I chose to be a theologian I would fight my way through to a position which I think a priori would be congruent with the faith of my fathers. I am impatient of those who in effect want to shape God so as to be convenient to their own position at any particular point. However I am patient with those who view God as continually mysterious, as a God who on the one hand will not, cannot in fact, suspend His guarantees to the human race as they were received and have been communicated to us, but on the other hand, a God whose idea of history and the rhythms of history may well be inscrutable. By which I mean such mundane things as this, that if God chose to help us at this moment, by let's say giving us one spectacular, highly visible miracle, I would be enormously grateful to Him in this age when faith is faltering. But it may very well be that the mood is not right and that God feels that it would be over-obliging to assert Himself at a moment when the human posture is not ready for Him.

1

## II. CALLAHAN

I do not believe in, nor have I any interest in, the transcendent or immanent God of the Christian tradition. Such a God seems to me rationally implausible, a threat to Christian values and an offense to morality. The latter two points are most important, but a word should be said on the first. I believe the idea of "transcendence" is meaningless, if taken to mean that which is totally other than man and nature. I haven't the faintest idea what something totally other could be, nor do I find the possibility attractive. I have never had any experiences of transcendence, other than the relatively routine sort whereby one imagines a kind of human existence superior to, but not radically different from that which one knows at particularly joyful moments of life. The sooner humanity ceases to lust after radical transcendence and a God who represents such transcendence, the wiser and more mature will it be. I am also singularly unimpressed by the idea that God somehow continues to reveal himself in history, or that he can be discovered in the depths of the self. I have not been able to discover his presence in history (except in the one instance of Jesus nearly 2000 years ago) and all I discover when I probe myself is myself and those other human beings who make me what I am. It is not that "God is dead"; he never was in the first place.

The moral objections are even stronger. If God is omnipotent, then he should use his power to lessen the evil which stems from human freedom. But this assumes he is all good; since he has not so used his power to lessen the evil to any noticeable degree, he cannot be all good. If he is omnipotent, but not all good, then he is a monster to be feared. If he is all good, but not omnipotent, then he does (as a concept) take on a certain interest. But not, for me, an interest of much consequence. There are, in that case, more significant things to worry about. Most importantly, the whole method whereby evil is excused in the world—as a fruit of the total freedom God gave man—seems to me monstrous. Christian morality would judge me harshly if I deliberately refused to save the life of a child about to run in front of a speeding auto. If I chose to save that child's life, no one would accuse me of hindering that child's freedom of choice; on the contrary, I would be judged as serving that child's freedom. Yet we are supposed to believe that, in the name of freedom, God has willed not to directly intervene in matters of life and death. But if it is immoral for me not to intervene in many critical situations in the life of another, I do not see why it should be less so for God to intervene. If this is God's idea of freedom, he can have it. I prefer morality.

Am I then a total unbeliever in "God"? I don't believe in a God of "mystery," a God men cannot talk about or have knowledge of, or discern directly and immediately. The whole concept of "mystery," so far as it pertains to God, seems to me intellectual rubbish. I could, on the other hand, believe in a God who, like myself, has a body, is a very limited mystery, can be seen, felt and touched—in a word, a God who is a material (even if glorified) body, who is A being who exists, who can be seen, felt, heard, smelled and touched. I think I do believe in this kind of God, but he is a God, I take it, who would be offensive to both the tradition and to the most radical contemporary theists. I am constantly amazed that philosophers and theologians go to such great lengths to show that God can't be like ourselves. Why do we hate ourselves so much? If we can learn the answer to that question, the quest for transcendence, which is a sickness, will come to an end.

## III. DEWART

Many Catholics appear to believe that although the advancement of human understanding is normal and desirable in every other respect, progress in the field of religion is to be neither expected nor welcome. Perhaps they suppose that development is a remedy for imperfection, and that to admit any evolution in man's religious belief (in any but incidental respects) is to accuse God, as it were, of not having told man enough of the truth in the first place.

This attitude is all the more difficult to understand because during its first five centuries or so Christian doctrine underwent radical and extremely rapid development, not only in the common understanding of the faithful, but even in the officially defined teaching of the Church. This is true with specific reference to one of the most fundamental Christian concepts, namely, that of the trinitarian, incarnate God. Again, during the middle ages, the introduction of startling novelties in the conception of God, notably those due to St. Thomas Aquinas, bears additional witness to the fact that the Christian concept of God has not always been static. However, since the end of the middle ages Christianity has generally speaking tended to exhibit deeper concern with the preservation of its past than with the cultivation of its present and the creation of its future. The opinion has become widespread that stability of doctrine is desirable in itself. The idea that we might improve upon our concept of God does not have common prejudice in its favor.

This is understandable in the light of historical circumstances, but it is nonetheless regrettable, in view of the vocation to the service of human perfection which the Christian Church believes itself to have been called to. There is, however, a foundation for the hope that this trend may be reversed. It lies in the extremity of the situation reached by Christianity, as the evils of its unwarranted degree of stability have accumulated. The survival instinct of the Church may now assert itself. If so, we may be entering a new period of rapid and intense development in the history of Christianity, indeed in the history of religion. This is the promise of the currently broadened horizons of philosophical speculation about God.

The Christian concept of God may well in the relatively near future develop in a direction definable by the following points. First, God is not to be conceived as a transcendent being, but as transcending being—that is, not as a being who is (by virtue of the very nature of his being) somehow beyond all that we could, on the basis of our experience, call being, but rather as that which is present, and gives ultimate meaning, to the being of all that is. If so, God is not a remote, inaccessible and absolute reality. On the contrary, the transcendent reality we call (as if by a proper name) God is close to being: it can be encountered in anything that is. Thus, however mysterious and inexhaustible, the reality which answers to man's religious quest is truly ultimate. There is no God behind the God of our belief: this is the real import of the traditional belief that God is uncreated. Hence, it does not make much sense (except as a metaphorical expression of the relations of man and God) to conceive God as inconceivable, or to speak of him as ineffable. Of course, the meaning of God, which depends upon our self-disposition toward him (that is, upon our faith, hope and love) develops—or should develop—indefinitely. But our progress, individual and collective, in our belief in God is truly an approximation, a drawing-near, to God—without the implication, however, that he is in the first place actually far away.

Hence, second, God is not to be conceived as having no real relations to creatures. But this should be better put the other way about: man's relations to the transcendent reality which we call God do not follow upon the absoluteness of God. Were it otherwise our relations to God would not really *follow;* they would be, as it were, the absolute beginning of our approach to God. On the contrary, our relations to God are strictly consequent: they follow upon God's prior relations to man. For instance, if (to use traditional terms) we owe certain duties to God, principally that ultimate and absolute self-disposition we equivocally call "love," the reason is that God has first put himself at our disposal; he has first made himself available to us. This is why belief is a response, not a call.

It is this prior relation of God to man which justifies, indeed requires, our dealing with God as if he were, like man, a center of consciousness, a person. For man's relations to God do not follow upon the disparity or alienation between what man is and what God is. They follow upon the interaction that actually occurs between man and transcendent reality—the initiative for which is evidently not taken by man, since he is not free to choose whether or not to come into being in a human situation that is definable in terms of man's consciousness of transcendence. However, these relations are truly personal insofar as they involve the exercise of our freedom and the creation of our personality.

Finally, God is to be conceived in such a manner that man's fundamental relation to him is that of responsibility. Man is the responder to God in faith, hope and love. To say that one believes in God is to assert that one plans or projects oneself as one's free contribution, as it were, to the cosmic process, to the history of the universe of being, in the presence of that which transcends being. Conversely, God is that historical reality to which we not merely pledge our intentions and our will, but for which we make ourselves to be whatever we decide to be, and in the light of which we understand ourselves in whatever way we conceive ourselves to be.

Thus, belief in the reality of that which justifies man's ultimate faith, ultimate hope and ultimate love, is not the same as the supposition that there must be a Supreme Being, because otherwise one would be deprived of the benefits of religion. It is a commitment to exist, consciously and by design, in a situation to which we contribute a self-concept definable by our consciousness of the fact that beyond the existence of all that exists there is a meaning which is not found in existence itself —a meaning which we grasp only to the degree that we ourselves rise above mere existence and in the same measure that we understand our own human nature as not circumscribed by its being whatever it is, but capable of transcending itself, even unto God.

## IV. FRANCIS

Nothing seems more incongruous to me than little men making their little boxes to package their little God. The very beginning of my concept of God lies in the fact that God being infinite I can never hope to totally understand Him.

But even if I can not wholly know God it is possible for me to come into a living relationship with Him. Those theologians who ponder over terminology, who say the language we use when we speak of God is faulty, miss the simple point—we are called upon to know God within the capacity of our finite knowledge but most of all to love Him and serve Him.

What is my affirmation? God is! I know Him in my imperfect way, I love Him in my imperfect way, my life when it is the life it should be is lived in rhythm and harmony with God.

I suspect that when I speak of living in rhythm and harmony with God there will be those who do not quite understand what I mean. What's worse, I don't know quite how to explain what I mean but I do know there are millions who will understand what I mean because their understanding derives from experience.

I don't mean the simple obeying of the laws of God. That is static. What I speak of is dynamic. I do not mean a God who intervenes in all details of human life—because God gave us free will. But I do mean a God who is concerned about all details in life, the God who knows the fall of the sparrow, who seeks out men and offers to all who seek it a living relationship with Himself.

I do not mean that a man who comes to this relationship with God thereby becomes healthy, wealthy and wise. He may well be closest to those who suffer in pain, who are the most poor, who are the fools in the light of the world.

When I speak of the rhythm of God I realize it isn't a word theologians use but it expresses what I understand. There is a way that men can come into a loving relationship with God in which their lives are lived in rhythm with Him. If they by their actions turn from what is implied in this relationship there results a discordance that will not be ended until they are in rhythm with Him again.

This is more than prayer, although prayer is a part of it. It is living a life in constant communication with God. Not consciously measuring each act but simply keeping in—well, rhythm is what I mean—rhythm with Him.

When men act in rhythm with God then what is achieved is far more than could ever be achieved alone, the happiness far greater than the sum of human experiences. It brings you a calmness in the world, an assurance that is deeper than human assurance.

Every man needs this, every man has within his soul a craving for this. There is a God-ache that would drive men to seek this personal relationship with God, a God-cavity in the very essence of man's being that cannot be filled without it.

It is the understanding of the personal relationship of man and God that I fear is being threatened today. There are men who speak in the fanciest terminology about God, who have all the right theological and philosophical terms, and yet have never come to a personal knowing and relationship with God.

It is this that turns men away from prayer and worship, acting as if they think the Christian life is nothing more than a kind of social activism. In an important way, being a Christian does involve you in action, but this action is organic. It does not properly exist by itself but it is engendered by your love of God. Action that is not compelled by your love of God is in danger of skittering off into futility. It is not connected to the source of power for the action. God is. I believe in God.

## V. MATT

Pope Pius XI, in his encyclical condemning Naziism, hit hard at the error, which has become more and more widespread in our day, namely, of considering God as some impersonal and indefinably evolving life-force. "The believer in God," the Pontiff declared, "is not he who utters His name but he for whom this sacred name stands for a true and worthy concept of the Divinity. Whoever, therefore, identifies, by pantheistic confusion, God and the universe, either by lowering God to the dimensions of the world, or raising the world to the dimensions of God, is not a believer in God. Whoever (substitutes) a dark and impersonal destiny for the personal God, denies thereby the Wisdom and Providence of God . . . Neither is he a believer in God . . . Beware, Venerable Brethren, of that growing abuse, in speech and in writing, of the name of God as though it were a meaningless label to be affixed to any theory, more or less arbitrary, of human speculation. Our God is the Personal God, superhuman, omnipotent, infinitely perfect, one in the Trinity of Persons, tripersonal in the unity of divine essence, the Creator of all existence, Lord, King, and ultimate Consummator of the history of the world, who will not, and cannot, tolerate a rival god by His side."

This concept of God, as expounded by Pope Pius XI and which is so clearly distinct from the "pantheistic confusion" inherent, for example, in Teilhard de Chardin's speculations about the "cosmic Christ" etc., would be well for Catholics to keep in mind nowadays in the face of all of the shallow theorizing and vague babbling so characteristic of the "God-is-dead" crowd. Reason itself tells us that God is no myth. Only an omnipotent Being who alone exists of Himself and is infinite in all perfections, could have brought forth heaven and earth and all things in it from out of nothing. The Apostles' Creed, not only emphasizing the fact of the three divine Persons in God, but the Virgin Birth of Christ and His suffering, death, and resurrection on the third day, reminds us that the Godhead is really distinct in reality and essence from all other things that exist or can be conceived, all of which, if they exist, get their existence from Him, "the first cause uncaused." Let us not, therefore, make the mistake so common today of identifying God and the universe, either by lowering God to the dimensions of the world, or raising the world to the dimensions of God. Either way we sin against the very first commandment of God Himself, who tells us that He alone is God and He will not tolerate any false gods beside Him.

## VI. SHEED

My God is the God of Jesus Christ. Having had a moderate training in philosophy (with some closer reading of the Phenomenologists) and an amateur's knowledge of the mystery cults and the world religions, I could carpenter an intellectually creditable concept of God for myself. Beyond admiring it, there is not much I could do with it. I would find it of no use to me if life were suddenly to turn serious on me—suffering and sin and such. Then I should be forced back to the God of Jesus Christ. My concept of God I have arrived at by using my mind (not intensely enough or continually enough, I admit) upon every word Christ said of God and what in his own person he showed of God; upon the statements in which the Church draws the present boundaries of its exploration, by thinking and praying and daily living of Christ's words; upon the insights of philosophers and men of other religions—all this illumining and illumined by, life as it has come to me. Had this book included a question about prayer, what we said about it would have told the readers so much about us—but maybe we shouldn't all have wanted to bare our souls—we are not all Augustines.

Certainly each man's experience of God is the vitalizing element. But there must be a wider experience than our own. Compare the creation stories of the great paganisms with the Genesis story—they are a whole universe apart, because the Jews had had the experience of God in the Sinai desert: we can have it too, in Genesis and from end to end of the Old Testament. And, to carry us at once deeper into it and beyond it, we have the Christian experience of God-made-man.

His Gospel is a gospel of life, life imperilled, life restored, life lifted into newness of life, and always *with God* from whom all life, all being, is. "Man *lives* by every word that proceeds from the mouth of God." "This is eternal *life* to know thee the one true God, and Jesus Christ whom thou hast sent." And the first rule of life, for us as for himself, is to love God with one's whole heart, mind, soul, strength. So that God is lovable, and God is knowable, since we cannot have so total a giving of self in love to one we cannot know. God indeed is love, so the disciple Christ loved tells us. Two other nouns we have after "God is"—the same disciple's "God is light" and Christ's own "God is spirit"— loving and knowing being spirit's specifying functions.

The Church has philosophised about God aided by Plato and Plotinus and Aristotle whom Aquinas baptized sixteen centuries after. Their contribution was God's self-existence, absoluteness. For them God's infinity placed him beyond personality, beyond the reach of creatures and not to be affected by them, in his immutability not reacting to them, in his perfection beyond care for them. But the Scriptures showed him affected by men, reacting to them, caring profoundly, loving so profoundly that he "sent his only begotten Son" (Jn 3:18), "spared not his own Son" (Rom 8:32).

The Greeks had not known Sinai desert or Gethsemani or Easter Sunday, had not heard of the Trinity or received the God-man Eucharistically. Yet there was true genius in their insights and their fascination is perennial, still operative on men who are convinced that they have de-hellenized both theology and their own thinking—so often one finds oneself saying "First de-hellenize yourself." With the Greeks, and with Zoroaster and Sankara and Lao-Tze and Heidegger, we can correct and clarify our concept of God, but not by throwing away his life, his love, his desire for an interchange of knowing and loving with us, his care for the smallest thing that lives. Your concept of God and mine may be not only inadequate because of our finitude but seriously misleading. But the way to correct it is by thought and prayer, a better living of the life Christ proposes for us—not by the moratorium on discussion of him that some men plead for, with God himself left nameless. That is the way to death, not life. There is indeed a silence which lies on the other side of speech, but it grows out of speech, after speech has enriched the soul with all that it has to give.

# 2. WHAT DO YOU THINK OF JESUS CHRIST?

## I. BUCKLEY

I think of Jesus Christ as exemplary and as authoritative. As I grew up I also found Him endearing, which I still do. I certainly don't find the God of the Old Testament endearing; in fact, my most recent mistake is to have started a moderately systematic re-reading of the Old Testament. It's emotionally a mistake; I find it impossible to fall in love with the God of Moses, just absolutely impossible. He was a horrible, horrible person, capricious and arbitrary. I am of course convinced that He was otherwise and I am sure that if I went to the proper exegetes they would explain to me how to understand Jahweh. But with Christ I had a very early love affair. It seemed to me that everything about Him was adorable. He showed every virtue, every endearing virtue—the capacity for passion, love, patience, understanding. And it is enough that He should have certified the God of Moses as being my God that I take His word for it.

I acquired a love for Christ through my mother. She is a very devout Catholic and somewhere along the line she developed a very personal relationship with Christ. It was communicated to us children so that there was never any doubt in my mind. He struck me the way He struck His apostles, as simply undeniable. Since reaching intellectual maturity I've always been on the lookout for similar reactions and I've found them. For instance, in such odd pieces of literature as Arnold Lunn's book *The*

*Harrovians*, where the headmaster, confronted by a boy who is tending toward agnosticism, says "but look, how could Christ have been a phony?" How could anyone who wasn't divine have been the way He was?

## II. CALLAHAN

I believe that Jesus Christ is true God and true man. He is true God because he continues to exist in a glorified body. He is true man because he continues to exist in a glorified body. In other words, he is true God and true man for the same reasons. As God, he exists in a glorified body, a body presumably free of the limitations we normally associate with bodiliness: pain, inexplicable finiteness, passion, aggression, and the like. At the same time, we may believe that this God-in-a-body is a God who can be seen, felt, heard, smelled and touched. In the figure, indeed in the concrete person, of the risen Christ, we have a perfect image of God. He is one like ourselves, only more so—I won't say infinitely more so since I don't know what that could possibly mean. He is different from ourselves because he has risen from the dead and continues to exist for all time; when we rise from the dead—if we do—we will be like him: a bodily creature, but now a creature liberated from the body of limitations. We have in the image of the risen Christ an answer to the problem of God: God is a body. We also have an answer to the problem of man: man is destined to be a risen body. Is Jesus our redeemer? Yes, for he redeemed us from being forced to think of God as an impenetrable mystery. Yes, for he redeemed us from being forced to think that man was ever guilty of "original sin." Yes, for he redeemed us from that self-hatred which has led man, in self-destructive futility, to seek transcendence. When will we accept this redemption?

## III. DEWART

Christianity's emergence from Judaism began with the belief that Jesus of Nazareth was the Christ, the promised "redeemer" expected by Israel—but in the novel sense that the man who was the Christ manifested, not at a distance, as it were, but "in person," the reality of God, his agency in the course of human events, and his unfailing self-gift to man, and in the sense that this self-revelation, fellowship and self-gift were effective not only now, but most especially in relation to the final outcome of human history. Later speculation about Jesus and his relation to God led (understandably enough, in view of cultural circumstances) to the formulation of the primitive belief in the Christ Jesus in terms of the union (in one person) of two natures, the human and the divine. For all its original advantages, however, this idea of the "incarnation" of God has entailed some difficulties, especially since the end of the Middle Ages, when in the effective belief of Christians the divine nature has increasingly overshadowed the humanity of Jesus. The disadvantages of this have been real and unfortunate, and they have been compounded by the sincere retention of orthodox formulae which affirmed something different from what many Catholics have actually believed.

This crypto-docetism and crypto-monophysitism, this unconfessed and unconceptualized belief that Jesus was God in the disguise of human appearances, cannot at this late date be remedied by any amount of renewed emphasis upon the reality and fullness of the humanity of Jesus. Protestantism has tried it, with results (if I may say so with full respect) which have been probably not more salutary than what Catholics have traditionally judged them to be. For the inadequacies of the fairly common understanding of the incarnation begin with the inadequacies of our understanding of God. If God is Supreme Being, truly a personal substance possessing eternity, omniscience, omnipotence, etc., then Jesus' relation to God must be understood as some sort of union of two things. Once the problem is posed in such terms, the idea that the "incarnation" is the personal union of two natures would be difficult to improve upon. And yet, it is of its very nature an unstable solution, in which either the divinity or the humanity must, despite every contrary outward affirmation, effectively predominate. Either the divinity is altogether denied, or else Jesus has no human personality—in which case it is difficult to avoid the consequence that in the human nature of Jesus God has impersonated a man.

However, if God is conceived less after the fashion of a man with all limitations removed, and if at the same time nature is not conceived as an inalterable and fixed structure which defines a being and its possible operations, the uniqueness of the self-manifestation of God in the man who was Jesus of Nazareth might be understood in a religiously significant way.

The intelligibility of anything intelligible is conceivable as the specificity of its history. If so, neither God nor man nor any reality have an inner structure which determines them to be once for all what they are. The epiphany or self-manifestation of God in Jesus of Nazareth is unique, but not because of the uniqueness of the metaphysical instruments or other structural devices, as it were, of which God availed himself in order to enact it. It is indeed essentially different from every other self-manifestation of God: it is different, for instance, from God's self-manifestation to human consciousness in man's transcendence of being, or from God's manifestation to the believer as he reveals himself in the history of man. But God's epiphany in Jesus does not have the uniqueness of a difficult technique: its wondrous quality has nothing in common with a spectacular feat ingeniously achieved. The uniqueness of God's manifestation in Jesus is the uniqueness of an event which affected man's historical situation in a definitive way, as it divided all time into a "before" and an "after" and thus introduced a final epoch into the history of man.

Hence, Jesus of Nazareth was, in a sense, a man like every other man—that is, he was a man in precisely the same sense as every other human being is a man, even to the point of being a human person and having a distinctive personal conscious life. But in the full humanity and in the fully human existence of Jesus God manifested as a matter of historical, not metaphysical, fact the actual, immediate and real presence and action of his very reality or "self". Thus, to believe in Jesus is to believe in

God, in such a manner that, for instance, to listen to him is to listen to God, to crucify him is to crucify God, and to be "saved" by him is to be "saved" by God. But all this obtains without the implication that behind or within Jesus of Nazareth there was another being, God, using a human nature for the purpose of putting across, as in a charade, his impersonation of a man.

## IV. FRANCIS

I believe with Peter when he said, "Thou art the Christ, the Son of the living God." I believe with the Council of Chalcedon that He is true God and true Man.

I find those modernists who say that Jesus Christ was only a good man, the best of all men but only a good man, suggesting a concept that to me is illogical. No good man could have claimed for himself what Jesus claimed for Himself—"Before Abraham came to be, I am." or approve of Peter's claim for him. It is irrational, therefore, to claim He was only a good man. If He were only a good man, then His claims would have been the claims of a charlatan. He was either a charlatan or He was what He claimed to be—not a good man but God become man.

This I believe and I suggest that it has always been the great question, the question Jesus asked Peter, "But who do you say I am?" I answer it as Peter answered it.

## V. MATT

No faith in God can long survive pure and unalloyed without the support of faith in Christ. "No one knows who the Son is, except the Father, and who the Father is except the Son and him to whom the Son chooses to reveal him." (Lk 10:22). "Now this is everlasting life, that they may know thee, the only true God, and him whom thou hast sent, Jesus Christ." (Jn 17:3). Nobody, therefore, can say, "I believe in God, and that is enough for me," for the Savior's words brook no evasion: "No one who disowns the Son has the Father. He who confesses the Son has the Father also." (1 Jn 2:23). Our belief in Jesus Christ, the second Per-

son of the Blessed Trinity, is briefly but nonetheless unequi-
vocally set forth in the Apostles Creed, among other Church-
approved professions of Faith. Accordingly, Jesus Christ is
infinitely more than an historical personage or extraordinary
human being who once inhabited the earth and became a shining
example to others. Jesus Christ, the second Person of the Holy
Trinity, is, according to our belief, true God and true Man, and
those who believe in Him and confess Him before men thereby
acknowledge also the Father in all of the Godhead's distinctive
attributes.

## VI. SHEED

Within the last year there was a dialogue in which graduates
of Catholic Colleges uttered their criticisms of the Church: the
report occupied twenty-five columns: the name of Christ was
mentioned three times and each time instantly dropped. Similar
signs of Christ's eclipse multiply daily—in books about the
Church's future which barely name him, in Catholics leaving the
Church unaware that they are leaving him and unconcerned
when they are reminded. We are moving away from Peter's
"no other name under heaven by which we must be saved"
(Acts 4:12); from Paul's "It is no longer I that live but Christ
lives in me," (Gal 2:20); from Christ's own definition of Redemption—"I in my Father and you in me, and I in you" (Jn
14:18).

The way back lies in coming to know the Christ of the Gospels—not know *about* him, but know *him*, make our own intimacy with him. It is of course the Risen Christ who is in heaven
interceding for us *now;* who lives in us and in whom we live
*now.* But in heaven he is not under our gaze, in the Gospels
he is; in heaven he is not living life as we live it, in the Gospels
he is.

The Christ of a thousand statues and a million holy cards,
who melts and yearns and does little else, will not stand the
Gospel test. But with this picture lifted down from the mind's
wall, what takes its place? It is easy to have Christ barely

more real than a figure in one of his own parables. The Gospels should remedy that too. We can hardly fail to notice that he speaks and acts on two levels—saying and doing things wholly human, but also things beyond man's range, yet using the same "I" for both—"I thirst," "Before Abraham was made I am." We return to the Church's doctrine of the Incarnation—two levels of action utter the two natures, the one "I" the single Person (person being seen as that which says "I"), the Second Person of the Trinity. Seeing Christ thus, the Gospels become luminous: reading the Gospels, the doctrine takes on richness and actuality.

He was true God, but not to any diminution or adulteration of his human reality. As man he was not omniscient, a created mind cannot be. He learnt as men learn: beyond that God gave him, as he had given the prophets before him, all the knowledge required for his mission. But matters which concerned him neither as Savior nor as Revealer—why should he have known those?

Nor did he start life with a body made especially for him, generations of ancestors had gone into it. He does not march majestically through the story of Redemption, he reacts not as Man-in-the-Abstract, but as that man, the man we meet, and make our own intimacy with, in the Gospels.

Every religious theorist has his own idea of what the God-man would have done, would have said. What they have to offer us we shall judge all the better for knowing what the one God-man did do, did say—which includes knowing what provision he made that we might know his mind.

# 3. THE TRINITY

## I. BUCKLEY

My view of the Trinity is that here one gets into a theological concept the meaning of which to a layman is not terribly important. I am very much against any defiance of the idea of the Trinity for the reason that it strikes me as more an act of defiance than an act which would result in a different understanding of the application of Christianity to the layman or even to the religious orders. I've never actually probed deeply the origin of the unitarians but neither have I probed the necessity of the notion of the Trinity. The necessity to understand Christ as divine and yet as "other" than the God who dispatched Him to earth, to Whom He constantly refers in the Bible, certainly sets up a necessity to understand Christ as participating in divinity. But the ultimate geometrical division into three parts is not something that ever engaged my attention, perhaps because I haven't done enough studying of the role of the Holy Ghost as necessarily "other". When I speak of Christ as participating in divinity, do not misunderstand me—I do believe that Christ is God. But in virtue of the fact that our own Euclidean vocabulary requires us to consider his "being" God as occupying the category of Godness, we are left with the requirements, as I judge, to use things like "participating in" or "being a part of" in order to leap over the Euclidean inhibitions. In other words, if Christ is God, then nobody else can be—but we know that something else is also and we know therefore that He participates in Godness. But I don't mean to use participate in the sense in which some people use it, extending it so far as to say that you and I participate in divinity.

## II. CALLAHAN

I am tempted to say that the Trinity, like celibacy, is for those who can bear it. I do not know what to make of the traditional doctrine; it strikes me as wholly obscure, a mere way of playing with words.

If I believed there was such a thing as "God the father," I suppose the doctrine might make some sense. But since I don't believe in something called "God the father," even in that analogical sense theologians like to play with or in that symbolic sense sophisticated philosophers of religion knowingly foster, I can't even make a start on the Trinity. Once upon a time, I did believe in the Trinity; and I knew all the traditional reasons why I did and why I should. But I can't recall just now how it all went. There is only one God, and he is Jesus Christ. He is a father because he shows me the way to the light. He is a son because he is flesh of my flesh. He is a spirit, because he showed us what it is for the body to be glorified.

## III. DEWART

The trinitarian concept of God has been, of course, the most distinctive contribution of Christianity to the history of man's developing awareness of God. Monotheism was not simply the discovery that there is a numerically single point on which man is to focus his self-disposal, or that there is an all-encompassing principle by which man is to abide in his self-relation to reality. It also implied that such a point and such a principle were totally distinct from that which converges on that point and from that which is encompassed by the principle—in a word, that God transcends the whole of creation. God is the absolute which is relative to nothing else, and to which everything else is relative.

The God of Christianity, however, truly and literally relates himself to creation and, above all, to man—albeit gratuitously and without a prior claim on the part of creation in general, or of man in particular. For example, God's influence upon the course of human events is not exerted through deputies or intermediaries:

he is himself, in person, an actor in human history. He does not send messengers: he delivers his messages himself and, indeed, his messages are not propositions about himself. For his message is himself: God is truly and immediately present to man. Likewise, his benevolence to creation is not a love from afar: it is embodied in his animation of creation and, as it were, in his embrace of it. In sum, the Christian God so closely relates himself—in his very substance and reality—to creation, that his relativity to creation must be thought of as an integral part of him. Thus, God is, to put it paradoxically, absolutely relative. He is relative in himself, and not merely (as man is) relative only by virtue of the relations into which he actually enters.

The oneness of God is not, therefore, that which makes him an extremely rare substance. On the contrary, it is that which makes him abundant and even commonplace. All being has its being "in" God, who is, as St. Paul put it, "all in all." The doctrine of the Trinity asserts that, for all his transcendence, God may be conceived in terms of his relations to creatures, because to communicate himself, to impart himself and to relate himself are not superadditions to his reality, but *are* his reality: *Deus caritas est.*

In early Christian times this conception of God was expressed, in the paradox that God was both one and threefold (*uno et trino*). This paradox was made viable by means of a distinction between "person" and "nature." This was a helpful way of conceptualizing the Christian belief against the background of the hellenic culture. But having become subsequently frozen in this conceptual mould, the doctrine has lost meaningfulness to the very degree that common experience has been influenced by cultural evolution. It stands, therefore, in need of redevelopment.

## IV. FRANCIS

I believe in the Trinity. My belief is logical. I believe the Catholic Church is the Church founded by Jesus Christ and guided by the Holy Spirit. I believe the Scriptures are the word of God.

The Catholic Church has taught belief in the Trinity through the centuries of the Church's existence. There is clear evidence of the teaching of the Trinity in the Scriptures.

Therefore, I must through logic believe in the Trinity since it is a belief taught by the Church and found in the Scriptures.

I do not comprehend the Trinity. I had thought at first that I might state some of the ways that I gain some apprehension of the meaning of the Trinity but then I thought again that these are really not pertinent observations. My belief is not dependent on them, they may bolster and tend to substantiate me in my belief but my belief is the logical result of my belief in the Church and in the Scriptures.

I do not wonder that men, if they try to reduce the concept of the Trinity to their own observation and experience, would find difficulty with the idea of the Trinity. That's what comes of trying to put God in a box. If you try to box in God in a box of finite dimensions you simply can't succeed. You wind up with something other than God in your little box, perhaps a God made in the image of man. The concept of the Trinity is not boxable but I do not doubt it.

## V. MATT

The Most Holy Trinity consists of the three Persons—Father, Son and Holy Ghost—in one and the same God. God is one in nature, but in that one God there are three distinct Persons—the Father, the Son who proceeds from the Father by generation, and the Holy Ghost who proceeds from the Father and the Son as from one principle, by spiration.

## VI. SHEED

God is mystery, in the sense that we cannot know him as he knows himself. It is not that he wants to be hidden and jealously guards himself from our gaze. His mystery is invitation, not exclusion: the limitation of vision lies in our finiteness. God is love, and love fulfilled in union; love longs to know and be known. In the revelation of the Three-in-One, God gives the ultimate proof of love, for he lays his innermost life open to us.

He has made us in his own image and likeness: our highest powers—to know and to love—image him so far as the nothing of which he created us can image him. Our knowing and loving are productive; his too, but infinitely. His knowing produces an Idea of himself, as mine of myself. But his Idea is wholly adequate, lacking nothing that is in himself, eternal and infinite as he is— not something as ours is, but Someone, a Self, the Word, the Son —One who both knows what infinite love is and can return it. In love they utter themselves wholly. And the love in the Godhead is not less productive than the knowledge: from it too proceeds a Someone, a third Self, the Holy Spirit. Each is wholly himself, wholly God. Yet God is one God, as I with my knowledge and love am one man.

His revelation meets two resistances, a religious and a non-religious one. The religious one we find all through human history —an adoration of the Mystery, adoring God for his incomprehensibility, adoring incomprehensibility to the point of holding that within the Godhead there is an area which is dark even to God. Short of that extreme, the tendency is all about us now. It is a reaching back to the Old Testament God, known only in his action upon men, in himself unknowable: as though with the veil of the Temple rent, the old awe still held men back. But Christ invites us deeper in to the Holy of Holies than High Priest ever went, and more of God was hidden for Isaias than for us.

The non-religious resistance to the Trinity is different—part of the demand for relevance. As though one said to Christ "All this is very interesting no doubt, but its only about *you*. What difference does it make to *me?*" This attitude could not co-exist with love—but I read acres of modern Christian writing without coming across any reference to God's love. When we get the question put bluntly, we simply say "Try it and see," a reasonable answer in a world which—rightly—prices experience so high. And close on fifty years of talking of God in thousands of outdoor meetings have shown crowds fascinated by the doctrine, finding light and nourishment in it as in no other.

# 4. THE VIRGIN BIRTH OF JESUS

## I. BUCKLEY

*Ante partu, in partu, post partu.* It's the post partu that's difficult, isn't it? How far does *post partu* extend? *Ad aeternum.* In other words, it presupposed a continuing celibate relationship. I must say I just cannot understand why anybody would lather himself up about that. After all, platonic marriages are infrequent, but they are not all that infrequent. To suppose that there could not have been a coincidence between a platonic marriage and a marriage in which the mother mothered Christ seems to me awfully, well, provocative.

The questioning of the Virgin Birth seems to me to be a sort of post-Freudian attempt to hit back at any of the ancient suggestions that there is something in the sexual act that suggests that uncleanliness which traditional Catholic doctrine assumes is the carrier of original sin. That's how I understand it psychologically. That people should concern themselves about this is an effort to simply shout defiance at the notion that the consummation of marriage is in and of itself the carrier of original sin. As far as I am concerned the doctrine of the Virgin Birth is obviously an inference, it is not something that was subject to empirical biological confirmation. The question therefore arises if it is an inference a) is it reasonable, and b) if it is not reasonable, is it something nevertheless to be believed lest one defy the entire epistemological authority of the Church. My answer is that it is far more credible than a lot of other things that the Church chooses to declare as so, and that under the circumstances, it taxes me far less to believe in it than other things which I believe in because I am told to do so.

## II. CALLAHAN

My general reaction to the doctrine of the Virgin Birth is to think that it seriously compromises the more fundamental doctrine of the incarnation. One of the basic tests for the presence of a human being is his descendancy from human parents. If Jesus was true man, then it is logical to assume he had human parents; if he had human parents, then it is logical to assume he was true man. Either way, a full complement of human parents seems necessary, a human father and a human mother. If one of his parents was not human, then our warrant for claiming of him a true humanity is seriously jeopardized. He would, then, have a different kind of humanity than ourselves; and his value to us would, to that extent, be lessened. That the Church has seen fit to believe in a virgin birth suggests to me that the Church has been unwilling to grant full humanity to Jesus. The doctrine of the Virgin Birth, then, is a variant on the monophysite heresy.

## III. DEWART

It should go without saying, but it may be better to leave no opening for doubt, that having no authority to define what is and what is not the true meaning of Christian belief this writer can only state personal opinions, views which are no better (or worse) grounded than the reasoning which leads to them and the evidence on which they rest. This applies, of course, to every subject discussed in this book: I stipulate it only at this point because, more so than on topics which one would imagine to be more important than this (such as those already discussed above), disagreement with the traditional interpretation of Christian doctrine in this particular area is apt to excite deep feelings—even among those who have surmounted that cryptodualist attitude toward sexuality according to which it would have been out of keeping with the holiness and dignity of God to have taken in Jesus a sexually generated human nature.

I should make it clear from the outset that the Catholic believer cannot cavil at the fundamentalist reading of Scripture in this (or in any other) respect simply on the grounds that the authority of science forbids it. For the Christian cannot without self-contradiction place his faith in science or, for that matter, in any other form of human reason. On the other hand, faith builds upon ordinary human experience—which is rational in nature and which is affected, for instance, by scientific discipline.

The truth of faith cannot be conditioned upon the findings of science—but the findings of science can be reasonably arrived at only through reason, not through deduction from the truth of faith. Thus, any objection to fundamentalism should be based not upon considerations pertaining to the order of science, but to the order of faith—keeping in mind however that faith is a dimension of human experience.

Fundamentalism is objectionable because to insist upon any given conceptual, culturally concrete form of religious truth, even after such a form has ceased to be consistent with the current level of man's cultural development, is *religiously* prejudicial: it *obscures* the very meaning which the obsolete conceptual form once *revealed*. For example, to insist even today upon the accuracy of the mechanics of the process of creation according to Genesis would be to *miss* the point which Genesis presumably intends to teach, namely, a fundamental truth about the relation of man and of all creation to God. At one time this religious teaching could not have been imparted except in and through a cosmogony. Today, on the contrary, it cannot be adequately communicated except in abstraction from astrophysics and biology.

The Gospel accounts of the conception of Jesus from no human father, and his birth from a virgin, have in the past adequately expressed, against a certain cultural background, the doctrine of God's unique self-manifestation in the person, existence and life of Jesus of Nazareth. It would not seem reasonable, however, to suppose that the Gospel actually wishes to teach certain gynecological facts about Mary or to enlighten man about the embryology of Jesus. And to insist that God has the power to work miracles would be quite as irrelevant as to remember, with facile accommodation, that the process of parthenogenesis is, generally speaking, a perfectly possible if unusual natural phenomenon which may some day be artificially induced even in human beings. I fail to follow the reasoning of those who think that the conception of Jesus without the ordinary agency of a human father, and his birth from a virgin, both of these as physiological, biographical facts, are intrinsically connected with the divinity of Jesus—though I can understand why this should have seemed so in the past, and why even today it should seem so, if the real and total humanity of Jesus is not (despite verbal protestations and the retention of orthodox formulae) fully and effectively believed in.

## IV. FRANCIS

I believe in the virgin birth. I'm inclined to let my statement stand just there since I think it unnecessary to say any more than this. But I suppose since today there are those who question it, my statement must be a little longer than this.

A priest startled me during a discussion about a year ago—he was criticizing something I'd written in defense of belief in the virgin birth—by saying that he didn't think that acceptance of belief in the virgin birth required that you believe it was biologically true.

Well, if it wasn't biologically true, then it wasn't true at all. You can't talk of it as some kind of a poetic truth and expect reasonable and honest men to not scoff at you.

I believe in the virgin birth because it is clearly stated in the scriptures—I'm well aware that the account isn't to be found in all the gospels but that it is found at all convinces me.

Then I believe the Holy Spirit gives a special guidance to the Church and the Church has certainly taught the virgin birth consistently.

Now don't talk modern scientific knowledge to me—parthenogenesis is unknown in scientific circles but then it was unknown at the time, this is what worried Mary and Joseph.

I believe it and I believe it is vitally important. Theologians who relegate it to a place of unimportance, catechisms that ignore it, show a lack of knowledge of the development of theological aberrations.

Discard the concept of the perpetual virginity of Mary—something else I believe in—and you'll take the step toward discarding belief in the virgin birth. Discard belief in the virgin birth and you take a step toward discarding belief in the Incarnation. This isn't speculation, this is history.

## V. MATT

The doctrine of the Virgin Birth is that Mary, the Mother of God, gave birth to Christ, and yet remained a virgin. The Virgin Birth, prophesied by Isaias, Micheas, Jeremias, etc., and confirmed especially in the gospel of St. Luke, is an article of faith, by which we believe that Mary lived in perpetual moral and physical virginity, before, during, and after the birth of Christ.

## VI. SHEED

We hear it said that the Virgin Birth must not be understood biologically. But "Virgin Birth" is not a Gospel phrase. In the Gospels we have Mary saying "I know not man" (Lk 1:34), and the statement that Joseph "knew her not till she had borne a son" (Mt 1:25). It would be hard to interpret either phrase non-biologically.

These Gospels are the common property of all Christians; so is the Apostles' Creed which says that "Christ was born of the Virgin Mary." The widespread rejection of the belief outside our own communion is connected with the vanishing of belief in virginity, seen by most as simply a refusal of sex, a kind of anemia. To one who sees it as love given direct to God, there is no surprise in learning that when God entered our race He chose the gateway of virginity.

The Church sees her virginity as continuous. We find mention of "brothers and sisters" of Jesus, but they were not Mary's children

—cousins of Jesus perhaps as Jewish usage would allow. Whatever Mary and Joseph had in mind when they married they might well have seen that once the Son of God was conceived in her womb by the power of the Holy Spirit the ordinary way of sex was not for them. It is from the Jews that we have inherited the feeling that there is sacredness in things that the power of God has especially touched. The womb in which God's only begotten son became man is not for ordinary childbearing; and Joseph and Mary did not have children who would have been, not brothers but stepbrothers, second-bests at best.

Nor does this make a mockery of the marriage of Joseph and Mary. They were truly husband and wife, with a true union of personalities, a profound sharing of lives, each bringing a completion the other needed. They were both saints. If I may quote myself: "Sanctity is the right direction of energy, and the special energy it directs is the energy of love. Both loved God supremely, and it is not difficult to see their love of God pouring back in a great flood of love of each other, love so great that the ordinary manifestation through bodily union would have had nothing to contribute. There was more love in that virginal family, more married love, than ever a family has known."

# 5. INERRANCY OF THE BIBLE

## I. BUCKLEY

I just don't see how, with the intelligence that God granted us, we can believe that the Bible did not err. I take it as not only a philosophical postulate but also as a Christian postulate that the principle of contradiction is the cornerstone of our rational thought. If that is so, it seems to me that applied to the Bible, we do have contradictions within the Bible. Under the circumstances, the Bible has got to be understood through exegetes and this is one of the reasons why I suppose the Catholic Church was created by Christ, in part to guide us through the Bible. There are those who are impatient with the Bible's apparent shortcomings, as for instance I am and confessed to being a moment ago when I tried to describe the personality of Jahweh via the Old Testament. It seems to me that those who are that impatient might have ended up being more impatient if we had had to deal instead with a document which was totally rigorous in its implications and required absolutely only one interpretation.

It is true that we can find in the Bible apparently unambiguous directions, for instance the laws given by God to Moses, highly detailed laws as we all know. Yet these laws having to do with dietary businesses and how to respond to this kind of crime, etc., are defied every day by the Pope. I don't think the Pope can take Numbers or Judges seriously at all except as an allegory. And if he doesn't, he being my teacher, why should I? I think that the Bible has got to be thought of as numinous but not totally reliable as a sentence by sentence preceptor in all human situations. That, I continue to believe, is why the Church of Rome has so distinctive a role to play as the teaching institution.

## II. CALLAHAN

I have no way of knowing whether Scripture is inerrant or not. The only testimony we have which says it is turns out to be Christian testimony; but that is not enough to satisfy me. On the evidence, it clearly seems that Scripture is prone to many errors. The only way it can be saved from the evident fact of these errors is by devising one ingenious "higher" level of meaning after another. I am intrigued when I read the results of such efforts, but I am not about to stake my Christian belief on them; they are too obviously self-serving to be entirely trusted. On the whole, the meaning of Christianity can only be arrived at by means of a complicated interrelationship of the many sources of belief: an errant Scripture, an errant Church tradition, an errant conscience, an errant reading of the meaning of contemporary experience. Together they all add up to errancy, but an errancy which is relatively self-correcting. Scripture seems to me the prime source of Christian belief, but not the necessary or exclusive source. Taken together with the other sources, however, there is more truth in its errancy than men have any obvious right to hope for. Ours should be a "post-biblical Christianity," in recognition of the fact that there must always be a dialectic between the past and the present. Insofar as we take the present seriously, and thus the future, we must use the present to judge the past—in this instance to judge Scripture. Scripture will not always pass the test; but then, to keep the dialectic alive, we must let Scripture judge us— and we will not always pass its tests. The one option not open to us any longer is *sola scriptura*.

## III. DEWART

It is one thing to believe that the teaching contained in "what is written" is true. It is another to suppose that the writing itself, that is, Scripture, has the quality of truth. And it is yet another to suppose that what is true remains adequate for all time, that truth need not develop in its very truth and for the sake of its very truth. In brief, it is one thing to believe in God's self-revelation; it is another to believe in the Bible (or for that matter, in Tradition, or in both). One is reasonable; the other may be the result of some confusion.

Obviously, no one could seriously propose that an omniscient God can make mistakes. But it may be somewhat inadequate to think of God as someone who makes use of a medium of communication that is in itself subject to truth or falsity (namely, propositions) but who is at the same time so proficient at formulating them that he could make no mistakes. The belief that the teaching of Scripture is true insofar as God reveals himself in that teaching need not imply the validity of whatever is stated in the Bible on the grounds that God is its "author"—unless the divine authorship of God were understood in an impossibly literal way.

More important yet, apart from any question raised by the nature of the medium it should be noted that the truth of God's revelation cannot be understood to be the truth of an eternal fact: it is a truth-for-us. Therefore, our understanding of the truth of revelation enters vitally into its very being. To the degree that we become aware that beyond the adequation of the mind to reality, truth requires the ever more intense presence of the self to itself, inerrancy should become totally inadequate as a category expressing the relation between revelation and belief. Truth is not the adequacy of a representation, but the adequacy of existence. The ultimate truth is not the adequate representation of ultimate facts: it is the truth that decisively confers life, it is the truth that "saves."

## IV. FRANCIS

When this is interpreted to mean that everything in the Bible is literally true, I do not accept inerrancy of the Scriptures. I am certain the language is sometimes symbolic, sometimes poetic.

But this does not mean that I accept all of what passes as biblical criticism, either. A great deal of what poses as scriptural scholarship tends to eliminate mystery.

I think it is important for me to state that I do not look on the Bible as simply a collection of human writings. I believe the writers were inspired by God and I accept the Bible as the word of God.

For my guidance I will accept the official teachings of the Catholic Church, which existed before the New Testament was compiled, and on whose authority the canons of the Bible were accepted.

## V. MATT

Pope Paul VI not long ago lamented what he called new and distorted interpretations of the Word of God which proceed according to "whim or unaided human reason alone." Like Pope Leo XIII, he said that interpreting the Word of God in its fullest authority "cannot be done completely or satisfactorily except by means of the living magisterium of the Church." "It is absolutely wrong and forbidden," Leo XIII said, "to narrow inspiration to certain parts only of Holy Scripture, or to admit that the holy writer has erred." (*Providentissimus Deus*). It follows that those who maintain that an error is possible in any genuine passage of the sacred scriptures "either pervert the Catholic notion of inspiration or make God the author of such error," he said.

It is, in fact, the teaching of the Church—and this is an article of faith—that the sacred scriptures are free from all errors of fact and from the very possibility of error, since God is the author and God cannot be the author of error. The scriptures as originally written are absolutely inerrant therefore. Subsequent copies may contain errors of transcription but God Himself has prevented any serious corruption of the original text.

## VI. SHEED

Inspiration means—as a minimum—that the writers of Scripture wrote what God wanted written, and this would seem to mean absence of error. Yet there are numbers of things said in the Old Testament which are plainly not so. The New is different, inspiration being one of the "all things" that Christ "made new."

By "things not so" I do not mean whole areas of poetry, drama, parable, story which have their own kind of truth; nor certain accepted ways of speech, like the use of numbers as symbolical not arithmetical; nor the use of recognized literary conventions, as when Wisdom says its author is Solomon, eight centuries dead. I mean things stated as fact which are not fact, things prophesied as from God which never came to pass, like the blood-drenched destruction foretold for Babylon by Isaiah and Jeremiah. The word "inerrancy" seems to have a special meaning here which it has nowhere else. In Inspiration as in so much else God submitted his action to human limitation, ignorance in particular.

Today's scholars draw a distinction between things the writers are actually asserting and things they regard as merely accessory. This helps, but we come upon many passages to which it cannot comfortably be applied; and it can easily lead to the habit of writing off as not affirmed by the writer any statement that is proved not to be a fact, or even any statement that we personally find unacceptable.

It is possible that we have not sufficiently explored the phrase "what God wanted written." It is not unthinkable that God wanted many of the Scriptural books written simply as a true record of what happened, of the stages through which the human race passed on its way to the fullness of revelation in Christ.

The perfect statement on "inerrancy" has not yet been found. It may perhaps be on the lines of the definition of evil—the absence not of good but of *due* good, the good appropriate to, required for integrity by, a given nature. If we think of error as the absence of *due* truth, we may be less bothered by its presence in God's inspired word.

# 6. ORIGINAL SIN

## I. BUCKLEY

The thing about original sin that strikes me is that it is an explanation so brilliant, so ingenious, for what troubles us human beings, that if it had been intuited by others than theologians, the discoverer quite possibly would have been acclaimed as almost divine in his understanding. I just know no explanation for what it is that we face every day in our lives that is so illuminating as is the concept of original sin. The glory of Christianity is that it enables us to overcome original sin. I think original sin is something with which we are afflicted but which we can engage and every now and then feel that splendid sensation of overcoming. Even surpassing this is the strategic power of overcoming it to which we can aspire with the grace of God.

## II. CALLAHAN

Original sin, in its crude and literal version of an initial sin by the first pair of human beings, somehow handed down through the generations, strikes me both as a bizarre and inherently immoral belief. It is bizarre because it presupposes that God could stoop to some kind of childish testing of the first human beings. It is inherently immoral because it presupposes that later generations could be held responsible for the sins of the first generation; such a notion is repugnant to Christian ethics. By contrast, if the doctrine of original sin is meant to be a way of expressing the fundamental fact of human experience that we are prone to sin,

35

it makes considerable phenomenological sense. With Freud, I am prone to believe there is an instinct to aggression in man, an instinct frequently at war with an instinct to love. The concept of original sin, if taken as an expression of the conflicting drives in man—as the symbol of his finiteness—seems both profound and meaningful.

## III. DEWART

It does not take faith, it only takes some realism, to be persuaded that there is something wrong with man—I mean, not simply with individuals, but with the genus man. What is basic to the Christian faith is the belief that the absurd disparity between the abstract and the concrete possibilities open to man cannot be overcome except through an ascent to God. Progress will not remedy the generic condition of man unless it be progress in man's relations to God. Hence, the "restoration" of man to his proper condition is to be achieved only through the creation of a world made in the presence of God and decisively guided by the historical agency of God. To suppose otherwise would be to declare that man does not stand in need of God, and that faith has no essential place in man's evolving selfconsciousness.

The mythological form of this belief has been largely reinterpreted by theology in recent years. Nevertheless, the idea that there occurred at the dawn of human history a single concrete event which constituted "the Fall" remains widespread. It is implied above all in the belief that the restoration of man must be literally construed as a *return* (rather than as an ascent) to a human condition which actually obtained at an earlier point of human history. This appears to me as an unnecessarily fundamentalist belief.

## IV. FRANCIS

We get into many difficulties that are purely semantical. It seems to me that our understanding of original sin has often been defective because sin doesn't quite describe what is properly meant.

We come to think of sin as involving some culpability and so when we speak of an infant as carrying the stain of original sin we offer a concept that in view of the connotation is incongruous.

I know that proper understanding solves this problem but popular understanding often has not. I'm not going to suggest new terminology but I'd like to approach the subject from a direction that seems to me to give some insight into the reality.

When in the past we spoke of the stain of original sin we offered an imagery that was not true to the substance of the fact. What we have called original sin has never been something that is on the soul but something that is absent.

Man in his common parents received from God gifts that were not his by his nature. The enormity of that first sin of rejection is something that we can hardly imagine for, possessing preternatural gifts our first parents chose through pride to reject them.

Therefore, what could have been the heritage of all men was lost. What we have called original sin is therefore the absence of what we might have had and do not have.

We lost not only the preternatural gifts but we lost the communication of the supernatural in our lives. When through baptism we are restored to a vibrant supernatural life we are still not restored to the same state that God had given man but our first parents had lost.

What we are left with is a kind of God cavity, something that we all possess. St. Augustine in saying that our hearts are restless until they rest in God was expressing the reality of this absence of what we once had and remains within us unfulfilled.

We possess, to change the figure of speech, a kind of a God-ache in us, a sense of loss because there was a real loss. It is not only an absence we feel, it is a weakness that exists within our nature because it is deprived of what it once possessed. That it did not possess this by right but as a gift does not change the fact of the absence.

If we accept the concept through knowledge that comes to us

from revelation, it seems to me that it is an observable fact that this absence, this God cavity that remains unfilled except as we seek and come to communication and unity with God, is a part of the nature of man as he is now.

## V. MATT

This is the sin committed by Adam, the first man, eating of the forbidden fruit and in consequence of which all descendants of Adam, excepting the Virgin Mary, are born into the world with darkened intellects, weakened wills and a natural inclination towards evil. By the sacrament of Baptism men are restored to God's grace and life and again are enabled to attain life everlasting. This dogma, we read in the Constitution on the Church in the Modern World (Vatican II), though known to us by "divine revelation," also conforms with our experience, our awareness of our proneness toward evil, and our realization that the manifold ills surrounding us cannot come from the "good Creator" but are a consequence of sin. Because of Original Sin and its consequences, priests and laymen are exhorted by Vatican II to familiarize themselves with and live by those "moral and spiritual aids by which the temporal order may be renewed in Christ" despite the affects of the sin of Adam (*Decree on the Apostolate of the Laity,* ch. 2, para. 7).

In this post-conciliar era, when Pope Paul VI again sees fit (as did Pius XII before him) to condemn "any illusions as to the (so-called) natural goodness of man" (*Ecclesiam Suam*) and frowns upon various evolutionist theories, including polygenism and other hypotheses that would in effect deny the doctrine of Original Sin or even sin itself, it would be well to remember the words of Pope St. Pius X who said that "the starting point" for all enemies of the Catholic faith is the denial of the dogma of Original Sin and that from this denial "the entire edifice of the Faith, from top to bottom, would be shaken" and naught would remain of the concept of the supernatural! Vatican II reaffirms the fact of Satan and sin in these words: "a monumental struggle against the powers of darkness pervades the whole history of man.

The battle was joined from the very origins of the world and will continue until the last day, as the Lord has attested" (*Const. on the Church,* ch. 37).

## VI. SHEED

There has been a tendency to treat the Fall as the main element in the Redemption, with Calvary and Resurrection a postscript providing a happy ending. We have given Adam a prominence the Jews did not give him—the Redemption the Old Testament talks of is not from the results of his sin, and we never hear the Redeemer mention it!

Redemption itself, how Christ effected it, how it is to become ours, the new condition into which it brings us now and after death—these are the essential things; the Fall is only comprehensible in their light. We have to wait for Paul to bring Adam into the great sweep of the story of Redemption, completing the picture by his profound analysis of what mankind was redeemed from. If we start our exposition with Adam, we could be so caught up with the problems of evolution, monogenism, Old Testament scholarship, that we might never get to Christ's redeeming act at all.

Original sin means a sin at the origin of our race, which changed the conditions in which men must work out their destiny. One effect of it is that the birth which is ours, the life which is ours, as members of the human race, is not sufficient—we must be *born again* into a new kind of life by which we are made sons of God, indwelt by the Holy Spirit, capable of the fullness of union with God in heaven which is the goal for which God made us. Christ said: "Unless a man be born again of water and the Holy Spirit, he shall not enter into the Kingdom of God."

What of the sin at mankind's origin? Something happened then which, because of the solidarity of the race, affects every one of us in the way just outlined. But what was it?

The story is told by the man of genius to whom we owe Genesis III. He had certain insights as to what had gone wrong in man's relation with God; but with no knowledge of the detail, he uttered them in figurative language. The garden was a metaphor, how far were the gardener and his wife?

Did the first sin involve one man only? Does our involvement in the sin's effects mean that we are all descended from one couple. Paul seems to say so. Theologians, Scripture men, scientists are all at work on the question. I watch them with the liveliest interest; but meanwhile I know what Christ did about sin and what I must do about it.

# 7. HUMAN NATURE—CORRUPT OR NOBLE?

## I. BUCKLEY

I know that my answer is going to sound awfully ambiguous but the point is that nobility is an aspect of context. Read the last chapter of Malraux's book *Human Destiny*—it shows a murderous, thieving, assassination-minded bunch of people finally up against the grim punishment of Chiang-Kai-Shek's forces in the repressive Nanking uprising, and all of a sudden you find yourself admiring totally the protagonist who gives the arsenic that he had husbanded in the capsule in the bridgework of his mouth to a younger man who could not so easily endure the prospect of the terrible death that had been programmed for them, to be thrown alive into a steam engine. One might not say that this particular person was noble if one had surveyed his entire life—among other things he was an assassin—but he was noble at that particular point.

My general belief is that original sin commits you to the proposition that human beings are corrupt but that one must resist the Manichean tendency to proceed from that assumption on over to the assumption that man therefore can only act corruptly. What disturbs me most on the part of cynics and on the part of some theologians is those who go so far as to say that when you can detect an act of idealism or nobility on the part of an individual, you can explain it with some reference to the sexual urge of the moment or some act of personal gratification. There are those who would interpret for instance the act of that protagonist in Malraux's novel as an act of vanity and this I absolutely deny. I believe that human beings are, notwithstanding the fact that they are "corrupt," capable of sweetness. It is anti-humanism of the most perverse sort to assume that they are not capable of it.

## II. CALLAHAN

My response to this question is implicit in my response to the section on original sin. Man seems to me a mixture of the corrupt and the noble, if the question is to be phrased that way. Actually, I don't like the word "corrupt," which suggests a necessarily permanent state of sin and moral failure. I would prefer to say that man is both weak and strong, with the implication that his weakness is only a relative and not an absolute limitation.

## III. DEWART

In accordance with the view of original sin previously outlined, it seems to me that "corruption" and "nobility" are radically inadequate categories in which to cast our understanding of human nature in its present condition. For man has neither "fallen" from a condition of purity or nobility which he once actually had nor, on the other hand, remained in such a condition. Human nature is on-the-way, evolving towards a goal which is possible of realization, but which was not pre-ordained from the outset of human evolution: the goal is creatively determined within man's evolutionary history in the presence of a historically active God.

Thus, the ultimate perfection of human nature *may* be achieved; it will not be *inevitably* achieved. Man is *invited* or *challenged* to progress. Progress is normal to him insofar as it is required of him by the actual situation in which he exists. But human progress obtains through man's free self-creation and is, therefore, problematic. Human nature does not become ultimately "corrupt" or "noble" until it is "judged." There is no divinely pre-determined goal that man is required, first, to decode and, second, to conform to. Nevertheless, the outcome of man's self-creation is subject to judgment precisely as a free self-creation. The parable of the talents might be profitably recalled in order to illumine the conception of human nature as self-creative, within the process of a cosmic evolution which manifests itself to man as historical freedom.

## IV. FRANCIS

I don't think very often about things like this.

What a mature man understands is that when people do what comes naturally they don't always do what they would do if they did what comes supernaturally.

If you get to thinking of man as noble then you start expecting more from him than you are going to get. If you get to thinking of man as corrupt then you start expecting less than you have a right to hope.

Now it isn't just in being a Christian that a man can act nobly. Baptism doesn't make a man automatically noble and lack of baptism doesn't make him automatically corrupt. Some noble actions come from people who don't believe in God at all and some mean actions come from people who call themselves Christians.

Human nature is deficient, no doubt about that in my mind. So I don't throw rocks at a man because he acts according to his nature. It seems to me we should take man as he is, I don't mean being satisfied with this, just not being surprised by it.

At the same time, I know man is capable of great nobility and I keep hoping that he will act with nobility more and more often. The grace of God helps men to act nobly, although it doesn't prevent men from acting ignobly.

A fellow told me once he didn't receive Holy Communion often, that he would certainly never presume to receive the Eucharist every day, because he knew he wasn't good enough.

If we waited to receive the Sacraments of God until we were good enough to receive them we'd wait through all eternity. It is precisely because I am not good enough to receive the Sacramental graces that I seek them every opportunity I have.

Human nature, corrupt or noble? That's the question we were given and maybe I've strayed a little. Certainly my answer isn't deeply theological but then, as I said, I don't think often about things like this. Man is what he is and my personal observation of myself and my fellow man is that it includes a little of both.

## V. MATT

Human nature, though corrupted by Original Sin and by actual sin, has been nonetheless redeemed by Christ's triumph over death and thus has been raised by Him to an infinitely higher and loftier plane than the purely natural. "To the sons of Adam Christ restores the Divine likeness which had been disfigured from the first sin onward," says the Constitution on the Church in the Modern World. And the same Constitution adds: "Since human nature as He assumed it was not annulled, by that very fact it has been raised up to a divine dignity . . . (and) in Him God reconciled us to Himself and among ourselves (delivering) us from bondage to the devil and sin. . . ." Hence human nature, though corrupted by the sin of Adam has been ennobled and redeemed by the new Adam, Christ Jesus.

## VI. SHEED

Noble, certainly. But in each of us touched with, or smeared with, or wholly sunken in, corruption. Every one of us is a union of matter and spirit, by our spirit immortal, made by God in his image, and Christ died for our redemption.

Concentrate on one element in that definition—we are all made by God in his image, but in none of us is the image perfect. God is infinite love, for instance; we also love but at best finitely and at worst sinfully.

God created us of nothing, the formula for us is nothingness made into something and held in somethingness by the will of God; we can fix our love anywhere between God and nothing. We can fix it high and sink lower; we can seem to touch bottom and rise again.

God solicits us but does not coerce. And only God can judge us. But one vast compliment He has paid us. "Be ye also perfect as my heavenly Father is perfect." That is addressed to every one of us, which means that corruption is not of our essence. So nobility has it.

# 8. HEAVEN AND HELL

## I. BUCKLEY

Let me tell you one of my favorite little anecdotes. My friend Ralph de Toledano, a Jewish Christian, recently wrote a novel in which the words Heaven and Hell appeared and he capitalized them. They came back from the editor in lower case so he put them back in upper case. They went into print and he received the galleys and he upper cased them again. Finally he got a call from his exasperated editor who said "why are you capitalizing Heaven and Hell?" Ralph said "well, because they are places, like Scarsdale." I grant the probability that Hell is not a place in which the devil is required to maintain a Fahrenheit temperature of 220°, or that Heaven is not a place of pink clouds and those fat little winged cherubs, but I don't doubt that there are two conditions, two posthumous conditions, one of them a condition of desolation and the other a condition of joy.

What does personally disturb me about what is axiomatic in Christian theology is the notion that one cannot move from the one to the other condition, that grief and penitence and contrition in the next world are not efficacious. That disturbs me greatly. I don't know how to work my way out of that disturbance. But I have long since told myself that as a Christian I must not necessarily seek to be able to work my way out of that disturbance naturally. Then occasionally I remind myself of a tiny little anecdote told by a Jesuit who was giving us a retreat when I was in school in England as a boy. He said that an old dowager had come to him and said, "Father, let me tell you that when I die I will

45

not be happy unless Fu Fu, my dog, is with me in Heaven." To which he replied, brilliantly, "If it is true that you cannot be happy without Fu Fu in Heaven, Fu Fu will be there." An absolutely brilliant reply, from which I deduce a whole lot of things, namely, that if in fact the just position is one that permits effective contrition after death, then the just condition will exist, will prevail. If it doesn't prevail, it is because it is not just, and it is the limitation of our apprehension of justice that is at fault.

## II. CALLAHAN

The concept of "heaven" makes considerable sense. One likes to hope that man can look forward to something better than he knows in this world. I take it that "heaven" is meant to sum up and point to the reality which this hope tries to articulate. Beyond that, little can be said: we know nothing about what heaven is like other than that love will reign. In the face of such ignorance, one should remain silent.

The concept of "hell" seems to me immoral, if taken to mean a place of eternal punishment. It also seems to me immoral if taken to mean a place where those human beings who have freely decided to will evil, will for all time wallow in their choice. As a Christian, I would not wish this kind of fate even on a Hitler or a Stalin (or any conceivable moral monster). I can't believe that God would either. If he does, then I repudiate him.

## III. DEWART

The utter reality of eternal and irreversible "Heaven" and "Hell", as the outcome of individual and collective human historical creativity, can be trivialized by the fairly common insistence on their character as reward and punishment. But heaven is what man creates, individually and collectively, as the result of the exercise of his free existence in the presence of God. Hell is, of course, the opposite: it is what man creates when he effectively denies, in the course of his self-creation, the reality of God.

The wish to "go" to Heaven (and, of course, not "go" to Hell) is not only understandable, once Heaven and Hell are conceived as "places," that is, as pre-destined outcomes, or as situations already established. This wish is also religiously significant as an expression of good will. But, except under fairly primitive cultural conditions, the wish to "go to Heaven" and to "avoid Hell" is not very useful as a guide to man's creative imagination when faced with the task of disposing of his existence: it is about as useful as the maxim that good must be done and evil avoided. No doubt, there is an early point in the emergence of the individual human person, as in the evolution of the human race, when man's mere awakening to the moral dimension of human existence is to be considered a momentous discovery. This is indeed the root of man's conscious self-creation. But at the current stage of man's historical development it is not excessive to expect that adult individuals should rise to the awareness that morality demands more than the engagement of man's good will: it demands ever increasing initiative and creativity. The beginner may be given a passing mark, as it were, simply for trying hard enough, and for being aware that *something* is required of him: the time comes, however, when actual results begin to count.

Increasingly, as history unfolds, Heaven and Hell will not be conceived by conscientious believers as situations already created by God which merely await man's arrival. They may be better understood as ultimate situations created by man's arrival at *them.* It is perhaps unfortunate that the more primitive mode of understanding Heaven and Hell has been so generally retained by the Catholic Church, even as man is arriving at that level of consciousness in which he instinctively understands morality in terms of responsibility, rather than in terms of choosing the adequate means to appointed ends. For many, finding the traditional idea of Heaven and Hell to be infantile (as indeed anthropologically speaking it is), may also reject altogether the truth of the matter. And yet, in a very real sense the man of faith must constantly keep in mind "Heaven" and "Hell"—that is, the ultimate alternatives of the success or failure of free existence—in order to heighten his sense of moral responsibility.

## IV. FRANCIS

I believe in the existence of both heaven and hell—I recommend only the former.

Now beyond this I have not developed my concepts very far. My reading of scripture suggests they exist both as a state and a place. I am not bothered at all about the existence as a state, my understanding of how they can exist in a place is hazy but I don't doubt it. Nor does it concern me much; I do not doubt the existence of heaven and hell and in just what manner they are realized doesn't concern me at the moment.

I believe not only in heaven but I believe those in heaven are our witnesses, that they can somehow hear us asking for their prayers of intercession. I believe in heaven as much as I believe in earth, at least.

I do not doubt the existence of hell. Just what it will be like I do not know and I do not care to get any direct information. I'm certain nobody goes to hell unless he chooses to go there.

When I was a little boy I wrote in my third grade reader, "Dale Francis is my name. Troy, Ohio, is my station. To be good is my aim and heaven's my destination."

That's about the way I feel about it now.

## V. MATT

I have been taught since childhood and have never had occasion to disbelieve that heaven is the abode of God and of the blessed, where souls that have died in Christ's grace, will be forever united with the Holy Trinity in perfect bliss and satisfaction, and will share companionship with Our Lord, the Blessed Virgin and all the angels and saints. To partake of heaven's delights is to partake of everlasting life, to conquer sin and death itself in and with and through Christ's triumph over death on the Cross. "For God has called man . . . so that with his entire being he might be joined to Him in an endless sharing of a divine life beyond all corruption . . . Hence to every thoughtful man a solidly established faith provides the answer to his anxiety about what the future holds for him . . . heaven, eternal bliss, intimate communion with God," provided he obeys the Commandments and cooperates with the graces God gives to him. "Truly, the people of God have no lasting city here below, but look forward to one that is to come." (*De Ecclesia,* Nov. 1964, ch. VI, para. 44). The Church, to which we all are called by Christ and in which we acquire sanctity through the grace of God, "will attain its full perfection only in the glory of heaven" (*De Ecclesia*) when all created things will be restored and re-established in Christ.

*HELL:*

The abode of the damned, or place of torment, where souls that have died in sin dwell for all eternity. That there should be severe punishment for those who have willfully defied God and broken His commandments while on earth, or who have shown no love either for Him or for their neighbors, seems only reasonable and right. Somewhere, if not in this world, there must be a separate place or state both for reward as well as punishment. For before we can hope to reign with Christ in glory, all of us must appear "before the tribunal of Christ, so that each one may receive what he has won through the body, according to his works, whether good or bad," and at the end of the world "they who have done good unto resurrection of life, but those who have done evil unto resurrection of judgment."

## VI. SHEED

Death is a gateway. To what? The answer depends on what we love. If we love God and our fellow man, then this love will grow to its plenitude; if we love self to the refusal of love of God and man, then this refusal will issue in total frustration. The first is heaven, the second is hell: as to which it shall be, each man's will is decisive.

The New Testament has four statements about the life of heaven—all express it as "seeing." Christ speaks of the angels who "see the face of my heavenly Father continually (Mt 18:10).

St. John says "we shall see him as he is" (1 Jn 3:12). St. Paul says "Here we see obscurely as though in a mirror, but there face-to-face" (1 Cor 13:12), and "while we are at home in the body we are away from the Lord, for we walk by faith not by sight" (2 Cor 5:6-7). Seeing God direct, loving him at the new level of seeing, every element energizing at the highest, we shall at last be complete men, not as we now are—the raw material out of which men are to be made. Loving God flows into loving all that God loves, which includes all men—*all* men, from mankind's beginning none will be excluded save those who have refused. Just as the God of the individual is to grow to full perfection as a man, so the God of the race is to grow to full perfection as a community.

We may feel that we could do with something less splendid, more earthy so to speak, clinging to eternal retardation at our present level of development. Here on earth we cannot picture to ourselves what life at this next stage of our development will be. There is no diagram or blueprint. But we have Christ's promise that it will be wholly happy—"Enter into the joy of my Father."

A word on Hell. Christ taught its reality and its possibility for men—three times we read of his quoting Isaiah's last verse—"Their worm shall not die and their fire shall not be quenched." The Church's official teaching adds no detail. The essential hellishness of hell is in the refusal of God. Men need God as the body needs food and water. If they choose self to the refusal of God the result *must* be suffering, for self is insufficient. We can but theorise about the suffering, we cannot know—only that at its heart is frustration.

# 9. SATAN IN PARTICULAR AND ANGELS IN GENERAL

## I. BUCKLEY

Satan I think of as being literarily useful, but beyond that I think of him as the person we ought mostly to consider as being in charge of this world. I don't know how better to understand Christ's being taken to the mountain top and offered the kingdoms of this earth than to assume that it was Satan's to offer. I do think of Satan as being an expression for worldliness. When we say that Satan roams through the world seeking the destruction of souls, I understand that to mean that the allure of the fleshpots of this world is so great as to constantly be attempting to engage our attention over against grander spiritual pursuits.

The angels are presumably there as emissaries of the other world. Once again, the anthropomorphic Renaissance idea of the angels as pretty little people with wings who flutter about and help you at critical moments is something for which I have less than the fashionable contemporary contempt. I don't know what it is or who it is or how it is but somehow there are transmissions at odd points in one's life than one likes to think caused us to reconsider.

I don't think it matters whether we consider Satan as a symbol or as a person. There is a line in Milton "who and what art thou, O execrable shape that darest, though grim and terrible, advance thy miscreated front athwart my path beyond the gates." Of course, Milton was the sublime architect of the anthropo-

morphic view and I just don't think it matters whether you consider Satan as a "person." I don't even know what a person is in
this context. Satan is a force, and whether it is a willful force,
whether it is a force that can choose its targets, I don't know.
We must believe that it did choose its target in attempting the
impossible, the temptation of Christ. It attempted successfully to
seduce Faust, and the whole Faustian ordeal on which a lot
of western culture is based presupposes at least that Satanism is
visible and active, that it is reifiable.

## II. CALLAHAN

I cannot for a moment take seriously the idea that there exists
a fallen angel called "satan." No doubt it would be possible to
give some sophisticated explanation of the meaning and per-
sistence of this belief, but that kind of project strikes me as a
waste of time. Better that we just dispense with Satan altogether. As for angels, it is time we did away with them also.
How anyone could ever have believed in the existence of angels
is beyond me.

## III. DEWART

From earliest times Christians believed that Jesus was not a
messenger from God, but God's immediate self-manifestation.
God's institution of the appropriate human order was not medi-
ated by a decree or message from God, but by God's immediate
presence to man as embodied in the life, the existence and the
acts of Jesus, the Christ. Of its very nature, thus, Christianity
was bound to temper the early belief of the Old Testament in
divine visitations through "messengers," and it was logical for
the doctrine of such "angels" to develop into that which emerged
during the middle ages. In the doctrine of St. Thomas, for instance, angels are not primarily mediators between God and man,
but a sort of missing link in the chain of cosmic creation.

In my opinion it does make sense to suppose that man may

well not be the highest form yet achieved by creation. On the other hand, there is no reason to suppose that angels constitute a sort of parallel world, or that we are under the influence of such creatures, or that they play any role in the construction of the fabric of human history—least of all in the case of a malevolent angelic individual (or legion) who wages war against God on this earthly battleground for the stake of the allegiance of men and of mankind. Apart from the dualistic connotations of the doctrine of Satan, this sort of belief (which was surely understandable at a certain level of human development) tends to foment irresponsibility, insofar as it tends to draw man's attention from his own culpability, from the awful reality of his freedom and from the need for creative moral engagement in the arduous enterprise of creating the Kingdom of God.

## IV. FRANCIS

Since references in the scriptures concerning Satan in particular and angels in general are quite clear, I believe in their existence—if this is what is meant by raising the question.

It seems to me any examination of the scriptures would make it impossible to claim the references were only poetic or some sort of imagery. We quite clearly have the scriptures speaking of Satan and the angels. We have Our Lord speaking of our particular angels.

I'm quite well aware that this isn't considered quite modern. One man, having discovered I believed in the existence of Satan was shocked and he told me I should be aware of the fact that virtually everyone had discarded belief in the existence of Satan.

I told him that I hadn't realized Satan could be voted out of existence by popular referendum but that if it were true I'd not only be glad to vote him out of existence but I'd do some heavy campaigning to get others to do the same.

I not only believe in the existence of Satan but I'd like to observe that he seems uncommonly busy. As for the angels in general, I do not doubt their existence either.

## V. Matt

Satan in particular and the rest of the fallen angels are much in evidence nowadays when people, though scoffing at the dogma of the Immaculate Conception of the Virgin Mary, carry on as if all of mankind had been immaculately conceived and were in fact sinless, if not incapable of sin.

## VI. Sheed

### A. Angels

Angels have never been a problem to me. Man is a union of matter and spirit. There are beings who are matter only, why not beings who are spirit only? True, one can see the one sort and not the other, but it would be odd if the limit of our seeing were the limit of being.

Both Testaments are full of angels. One has heard them explained away as intruders from Assyrian or Babylonian mythology, taken literally by the Jews of long ago, but by us to be seen only as ways of personifying God's actions among men.

Christ himself did not take angels so. We are not to despise the unlearned, he says, for "their angels see the face of my heavenly Father continually" (Mt 18:10). It fits this when *Hebrews* says "What are they, all of them, but spirits apt for service, whom He sends out when the destined heirs of salvation have need of them?" (11:14).

### B. Satan

Among Christ's twenty-five healing miracles, six involve the casting out of demons. These too we hear explained away—he was simply falling in with Jewish beliefs when he appeared to take demons seriously. If so, he carried the fiction rather far—speaking to them, granting a request by them, ordering them to silence about himself. In any event this explanation misunderstands Christ as teacher—he would never have used a way of speech, however ordinary, that was based on, and would give currency to, religious error.

The mood of the moment is to flick Satan aside. He was not so dismissed by Christ, who called him "a murderer from the beginning, a liar and the father of lies" (Jn 8:44). He is woven inextricably into the story of Christ's redeeming death. He moved Judas to betray him, the High Priests to decide upon his death. With Calvary coming closer, Christ is continually conscious of him.

On the Wednesday before his death, he says, "now is the judgment of the world; now shall the Prince of this world be cast out" (Jn 12:31). At the Last Supper we hear him speak three times of the conflict, now come to its crisis, between Satan and himself, beginning with "The Ruler of this world is coming, he has no power over me (Jn 14: 30). But he warns the Apostles that Satan is by no means powerless over them. "Satan has desired to have you that he might scatter you through his fingers like wheat"—and he says that Peter is to be his answer to Satan (Lk 22:31). On the Damascus road, Christ tells Saul he will send him to the Gentiles "to open their eyes that they may be converted from Satan to God" (Acts 26:18). Which prepares us for John's summarization of Christ's work—"If the Son of God was revealed to us, it was that he might undo what the devil had done" (1 Jn 3:8).

Paul tells the Ephesians (2:2) that this same "prince of power of the air" is still at work. I see no reason whatever to think he is not at work now.

# 10. INFALLIBILITY OF THE POPE

## I. BUCKLEY

Yes, I do believe in the infallibility of the Pope, I believe in it as an act of faith. Whether or not it was wise to crystallize that doctrine in 1870, I don't know. Also I don't know what is left of the doctrine at the moment when people are apparently disagreeing on the question of whether a particular pronouncement of the Pope is is fact protected by infallibility, whether it is said with that due gravity the Pope must invoke when making infallible pronouncements. Put it this way, you can find two learned Catholics of whom one will say such and such a position uttered by the Pope is infallibly uttered and the other will say no, not at all, there simply wasn't the attendant majesty, the attendant formula necessary for an infallible pronouncement. I do believe that it is prudent to take the skeptical position in such arguments. By that I mean unless the Pope makes it unmistakably clear, as was done for instance on the question of the Assumption of the Blessed Virgin Mary, that this is intended to be infallibly true, it is prudent to suppose that an infallible pronouncement was not intended.

## II. CALLAHAN

I am willing to believe the Pope is infallible, but do not happen to believe it at present. The trouble is that hardly anyone in the Church really seems to believe it, except in a rhetorical way, and thus it becomes hard for me to place much credibility in the doctrine. The only evidence that the Church really believes in it—and then not the whole Church but only the magisterium —are a few short passages in the teachings of the First Vatican Council and a reiteration of that teaching in the Constitution on the Church of the Second Vatican Council. And that is not enough to convince me that the Church really takes it very seriously. Recent popes, for instance, have rarely spoken in such a way as to make it clear they intended to speak infallibly; on the contrary, they seem to speak in such a way as to allow one to construe their words as non-infallible. This practice suggests that the popes' own assent to the doctrine is notional and not real (to use Cardinal Newman's terms). As for the theologians, there seem to be very few willing to say exactly which papal statements count as unmistakably infallible; they continually hedge, thus depriving the doctrine of any real practical meaning.

I can only conclude from the practice of the Church, and the practice of the magisterium, that the doctrine is meant to function in some symbolic way; it is not to be taken literally. In any event, it is a doctrine shot through with logical difficulties. I would have to be infallible myself to know that the Pope had spoken infallibly, and so would every other member of the Church; but I am not infallible, so I could never know. Of what use is such a doctrine? None that I can see.

## III. DEWART

If one believes that the Christian doctrine is true, then one must logically believe that the Christian Church can be reliably counted upon, particularly in the sense that its teaching does not lead man astray: the Church is the source of faith, that is, the source of that upon which we may rely and trust. And insofar as the papal teaching office remains the principal authoritative teaching office of the Church, the expression "infallibility of the Pope" is not altogether lacking in good sense and credibility. On the other hand, a teaching which does not lead ultimately astray, lacking all truth and validity, may nevertheless be far from adequate to the needs of a specific situation. The conceptualization of this belief in the very terms "infallibility of the

Pope" is one of the best instances of this: it has naturally tended to solicit belief in the guaranteed nature of the wisdom, perceptiveness, good judgment, effectiveness and prudence of the papal magisterium. These qualities are, of course, not remotely guaranteed in principle, and are occasionally lacking in point of historical fact.

For the belief in the ultimately unfailing nature of the Christian faith does not itself provide any assurance—not only because the infallibility is ultimate, but also because it is dependent upon faith, of which it is the consequence and not the premise. Thus, it has nothing to do with wisdom or prudence; and it does not protect the faith but the community of the Church. It provides neither certainty, safety nor security—and insofar as it has naturally led to the opposite supposition it has been, in point of fact, misleading.

Thus, the "infallibility of the Pope," unfortunately so-called, does not mean that the teaching authority can in no way fail to serve and respond to the needs of the Church, or that it cannot fall short of what at any given time the Church should have grown to believe. It is but a minimal requirement of dogma. It may be unwise to assume that it is the most that should be expected of the magisterium of the Church.

## IV. FRANCIS

Before I became a Catholic, the very first thing about the Catholic Church that became absolutely logically clear to me was the belief in the infallibility of the Pope.

I do not think of this as some kind of a power that is passed on from pope to pope, I do not think of it as some kind of a magic that makes the man who is pope incapable of error.

The logic is that Jesus Christ, having established His Church, promised that the Paraclete would come to guide the Church in truth. Believing this, it seemed to me even before I became a Catholic that somehow the Church established by Christ would be preserved from the kind of error that would pervert or lose the truth.

Obviously a pope is capable of human error, there are demonstrations of this in history. I do not believe that everything a Pope says should be accepted as the word of God. While always seeking to conform to the ordinary magisterium of the Church, I do not expect that it will always clearly be infallibly true.

But in the essentials of God's truth, I believe the Church will be guided through history by the Holy Spirit and that the preservation of this truth will be guaranteed. Therefore, I believe that the Holy Spirit will preserve those men called to the office of pope from the kind of errors that might destroy that truth.

## V. Matt

On this subject Vatican II, in its Constitution on the Church, chap. III, declares inter alia: "All this teaching about the institution, the perpetuity, the meaning and reason for the sacred primacy of the Roman Pontiff and of his infallible magisterium, this sacred council again proposes to be firmly believed by all the faithful." Hence the same Conciliar document declares that "the college or body of bishops has no authority unless it is understood together with the Roman Pontiff, the successor of Peter as its head." It reaffirms (para. 22) the Pope's absolute "power of primacy over all, both pastors and faithful," and, whilst also upholding the bishops' "supreme and full power over the universal Church," it stipulates that this power can never be exercized without "the consent of the Roman Pontiff." "For Our Lord placed Simon alone as the rock and the bearer of the keys of the Church," says this same official document, "and made him (Peter) the shepherd of the whole flock." The so-called collegiality of the bishops, about which one hears so much nowadays, is decidedly restricted by Vatican II in these words: "This collegiate power can be exercised together with the Pope by the bishops living in all parts of the world, *provided that the head of the college (the Pope) calls them to collegiate action, or at least approves of or freely accepts the united action of the scattered bishops, so that it is thereby made a collegiate act.*"

As for the divinely entrusted prerogative of Papal infallibility—

i.e., on defined matters of faith and morals—the Pope's definitions, "of themselves, and not from the consent of the Church, are justly styled irreformable, since they are pronounced with the assistance of the Holy Spirit, promised to him in blessed Peter, and therefore they need no approval of others, nor do they allow an appeal to any other judgment."

Obviously, therefore, when Fr. Hans Kueng, or others of his peculiar persuasion, argue for more "democratization" within the Church, they are treading on dangerous ground!

## VI. SHEED

God gave his revelation because he wanted men to know truths which they could not know without it. If he had simply left the truths to take their chance of survival or misunderstanding or oblivion, as men produced their ingenious, multitudinous, contradictory interpretations, we should have been left wondering why he thought them worth revealing at all. Christ did not leave us thus wondering. He committed the truths to the Apostles, promising to be with them in their teaching till the end of time.

The formula with which he had sent out the 72 (Lk 10:16), "He that hears you hears me," was now universalised (all truths, all nations, all times) and brought to a point in Peter—who was to shepherd the flock when Christ ascended to his Father (Jn 21:15), and to confirm the faith of the rest when Satan tried to scatter them to the winds (Lk 22:31). We find no doctrinal authority reposed in the community as a whole to unsay what he said to the Apostles in general and to Peter in special, and no powers entrusted to them that met needs peculiar to the first Christians and not still felt by us.

In the body of bishops the teaching function, the magisterium, of the apostles continues. When they solemnly commit the Church and its Founder to a formulation of some point in the revelation, the Holy Spirit sees that they do not teach error: there will be further advance to be made since finite words cannot wholly contain the infinite, but what is defined is true, light-bearing. That is what infallibility means. And this infallibility, attaching to the bishops as a whole, attaches to one of them in special, the one who has succeeded to Peter's place. For what concerns us individually God gives individual guidance —light we need, strength we need. But as to the framework of reality which is the same for all there is this teaching meant for all.

Infallibility, we observe, applies to the exploration of Christ's teaching. To me it seems the minimum for sufficiency. If there be no voice to say "That is wrong," "This is true," then we have no way of knowing what Christ wanted us to know; we have such of his words and actions as are recorded in the Gospels, but as to what he meant, we have only our own choices among the guesses which fill the air. With no more than that, we are unnourished ourselves; and how could we take Christ's endlessly fragmented teaching to the millions starving for want of the food he trusted us to bring them?

With all I know about the sins and failures of the popes, I yet feel no temptation to envy other Christians their popelessness. Individual popes have varied from magnificent to mediocre to appalling but the justification of the papacy as an institution is what it has preserved—the great truths about God and man and the God-man, Mass and the Sacraments and the possibility of so rich a union with Christ.

# 11. THE ROLE OF MARY IN CATHOLIC LIFE

## I. BUCKLEY

What disturbs me most about the opposition to Mary is that it is so unchivalrous. That may sound like a dumb thing to say. Of course mariolatry carried too far is wrong—Mary is not divine. And I must admit I have never heard her spoken of as divine. But I have heard that some individual saints seem to have gone too far in thinking of her not merely as an intercessor but as someone who herself can reach in and affect divine-worldly arrangements.

Mary, it seems to me, is all of those things that the litany says about her. Admittedly it sounds sometimes awfully obsequious and it is also true that the cult of Mary has always gravely provoked a Protestant civilization. Kingsley for instance never tired of poking fun at Spaniards who fought like the woman they worshipped. But the special role of Mary the Church insists upon and I certainly go along gladly. She is not divine, but a veneration of Mary as the exemplary woman it seems to me cannot conceivably be thought of as in any way profane.

## II. CALLAHAN

As the "Mother of God," that human bodily God we recognize in Christ, Mary has an important place in Catholic life. She is a sign that our God was a human God, and remains a human God. But to say that she has an important place is not to say

62

that she has a uniquely special place. We should acknowledge her place but not dwell upon it. The very last thing we should do is ask Mary for her "intercession." If Christ is human, the very model of perfected love, we need no intercessors in approaching him. The whole concept of "intercession" seems an unfortunate hangover from another era, that of the fearsome and unapproachable monarch. It is a model of our relationship with Christ which should have no place in the Christian life. The less said about such things as "co-mediatrix" and "co-redemptress" the better; it is humiliating to think that a Church proclaiming belief in the Incarnation could ever have toyed with such things. Mary should be for us a model of faith and fidelity; that is her meaning, and that is enough to say about her. I have always suspected that one of the great attractions of Mariology was that one could build vast theological structures, with little evidence or documentation to stand in the way; but most of these structures were just pious speculations, usually reflecting certain cultural ideals and dressed up to appear theological. The Church seems now to have gotten away from this—an eminently healthy development.

## III. DEWART

Many Christian doctrines have been trivialized. But those which have to do with Mary have fared worse, having been saccharinized, sentimentalized and all but technicolorized. More's the pity, given Mary's importance to the Christian faith—an importance which is indeed difficult to exaggerate, but which is all too easily misunderstood.

Mary (and may I suggest that the simplicity of her unadorned name is the only fitting tribute to her memory which good taste should in the matter of titles allow) is, even in a sense more aptly than Jesus himself, the symbol of man's historical freedom. For the Incarnation did not, of course, depend upon the prior agreement of Jesus to lend himself to it—but it did depend upon Mary's humble initiative. She is, therefore, a model of man's responsible creation of history in the presence of God, a model surpassed only by that of Jesus in Gethsemane, whose responsible creativity was now fulfilled under the sign of conscious awareness of the consequences of his free actions. For this reason it cannot be denied that Mary could be truthfully called "corredemptrix of the human race."

However, the idea of continuing the traditional silly devotions and of dreaming up new honorific titles—even the style of which is reminiscent of the Augustan Senate's treatment of Livia—cannot be envisaged without the thought coming to mind that vanity does not cease to be vulgar and ridiculous simply because it takes a vicarious form.

## IV. FRANCIS

Since God chose Mary out of all generations to be the mother of His only-begotten Son there is no honor that we can pay her that compares to the honor that God paid her.

At the marriage feast at Cana, when the wine had run out they came to Mary. She told her Son. He said the time for Him to act publicly had not yet come, that this wasn't something that concerned Him. But she told them to do as Jesus told them. So, although He clearly did not wish to do so, He performed the first miracle of His public life.

In this I find a pattern for the role of Mary in Catholic life. Those in need came to her, asking her intercession. Jesus accepted her intercession even though He hesitated. But Mary told those who came to her to do as Jesus told them to do.

The prayers of those close to God are good—we do not hesitate to ask the prayers of our friends of earth. The reality of Heaven is as certain as the reality of Earth. So I do not hesitate to ask the prayers of those in Heaven and certainly we know the prayers of Mary are powerful.

If this suggests a very simple approach to the question, I believe in such spiritual simplicity. Mary traditionally has played an important role in the spiritual life of Catholics. I do not think that there can be any Christian unity that does not include a great devotion to the one who carried God Incarnate in her womb and nursed Him at her breast.

But it would be wrong not to warn that there can be danger of excesses. If we cannot honor Mary above the honor already paid her by God, we can honor her Son too little. If proportionately our spiritual life is centered in devotion to Mary and directed too little to Christ, then we are wrong.

## V. MATT

Mary being the Mother of Christ and hence the Mother of the Church, she occupies a place in Catholic life which is second only to that accorded to her Divine Son. If, as we believe, Mary received the Word of God in her heart and in her body and gave Life itself to the world, then it follows that we must gladly acknowledge and honor her as being truly the Mother of God and Mother of the Redeemer. At the same time, however, and since she herself belongs to the offspring of Adam, she must therefore be one with us, though, having been preserved from all stain of sin, she surpasses all creatures, both in heaven and on earth. Where Eve sinned and lost Paradise for us, Mary by her Fiat regained it. Thus she becomes the Queen of all saints, and for us is a preeminent exemplar of what is required of all Christians in their earthly pilgrimage. The Church Fathers see her as used by God not merely in a passive way, but as freely cooperating in the work of human salvation through her steadfast faith, obedience, and willingness to render sacrifice, even to the offering of her own Son on the Cross. She is therefore, as the Second Vatican Council reaffirms, "our mother in the order of grace" who "cares for the brethren of her Son" who are still on earth, with the same maternal love and care as she manifested toward Him and His disciples while on earth. Tirelessly, ceaselessly, whether on Calvary itself, where she stood at the foot of the Cross, or at Lourdes and Fatima and elsewhere in the course of the centuries, Mary calls the faithful to her Divine Son and to His sacrifice and to the love of the Father. Hence the Vatican Council admonished us "that the cult, especially the liturgical cult, of the Blessed Virgin, be generously fostered, and the practices and exercises of piety, recommended by the magisterium of the Church toward her in the course of centuries, be made of great moment, and those decrees which have been given in the early days regarding the cult of images of Christ, the Blessed Virgin and the Saints, be religiously observed." For "just as the Mother of Jesus, glorified in body and soul in heaven, is the image and beginning of the Church as it is to be perfected in the world to come, so too today she (Mary) shines forth on earth, until the day of the Lord shall come, as a sign of sure hope and solace to the people of God during its sojourn on earth." (*Const. on the Church*, Nov. 11, 1964)

## VI. SHEED

Heaven and earth—it is all one world. Death does not divide, only refusal. Abraham and Isaac and Jacob are alive—as Christ said, God is not the God of the dead but of the living. To the thief in the hour of his death, Christ, in the hour of his, said "This day you shall be with me in Paradise." Paul could desire to depart, to be out of the tent of the body, and to be with Christ (Phil 1:23, 2 Cor 5:8). The next world is close to ours, in living touch with ours.

There is a movement among Christians to excommunicate the dead, *de mortuis nihil nisi nihil.* The New Testament does not thus write them out of the fellowship, nor does the Church: her liturgy is a hymn of two worlds interpenetrating, one life throughout, one stream of prayer flowing from end to end. In direct contact with the God who made them and us, those who died loving God and neighbor have not lost interest in their neighbors still on earth, Christ's second commandment has not become a dead letter for them. At every Mass we ask the Blessed Trinity to receive the sacrifice we are offering in memory of Christ's passion, resurrection and ascension and to the honor of his mother and the saints—"that as we honor them on earth they should intercede for us in heaven." They are still citizens of one world with us. The Church has often been accused of divisiveness, but in this matter she knows none.

A Catholic reviewer of *God and the Human Mind* was surprised at my finding Christ's Mother still relevant. But if prayer for one another has relevance, as the Our Father and the whole of the

New Testament show, then hers cannot lack it. In consenting to be the Mother of our Redeemer she has already done more for our salvation than anyone but her Son. And in any event she is relevant to Christ. A mother is not simply a mechanism to get a son born; the continuing relation is as rich as any our human condition knows. If we want only an official relation to him, then leave her out: but who wants only that? There have been Catholics who, to quote Newman, have said things in her praise which can be explained only by being explained away. But a true love for her, a true reverence for her can only bring us closer to Christ.

I do not always know what people mean by experience: I record my own experience that life would be poorer without such intimacy as I have grown into with her and her husband and certain other saints.

# 12. THE EUCHARIST

## I. BUCKLEY

The sometimes expressed view that the Eucharist is primarily a symbol of community and that it would be almost meaningless to receive Communion alone is a view that I reject totally and with enthusiasm. My own notion is that the relationship between the communicants and the sacrifice is not trilateral. It is not one at all that requires the community, the congregation. I am aware that historically the congregation took strength and purpose from numbers and from the fact of the congregation. But congregationalism is not, in my judgment, Catholicism. As I understand it, Catholicism tells you how you must deal with people lovingly and it certainly encourages a high sense of community, but it does not in my judgment include other people in at moments of high privacy between yourself and your confessor, between yourself and the Eucharist, between yourself and adoration. In fact, all the sacraments are individually vouchsafed, the exception of course being the sacrament of Matrimony which is vouchsafed to two people but only when they are symbolized as one really. Which is why it isn't possible for a single individual to attain the sacrament of Matrimony. I think it is also true that receiving the Eucharist is a highly private communion. The fact that it is done when one kneels side by side with other people does not in the least detract from its continuing significance when you receive the Eucharist alone, in let us say the death room or in the hospital, or if you happen to be the only person in attendance at the 6 o'clock Mass. So I utterly reject the collectivist notion that the meaning of attendance at the sacrifice of the Mass is heightened by the fact of other people's presence.

## II. CALLAHAN

The Eucharist, like the liturgy more generally, is important but not vital to the Christian life. There should be Eucharistic celebration, but not a Eucharist-centered Christian life (see my remarks on the liturgy). The meaning of the Eucharist is that our God, Jesus Christ, is a God of flesh and blood. By participating in Eucharistic worship, we emphasize our belief that the God of pure spirit is a God we have transcended: Now we have the courage to believe in a bodily God, a God who shares our humanity, a God who is no longer (and who never could have been) a "wholly other," an "ineffable" something-or-other. How is this bodily God, Jesus Christ, present in the Eucharist? His presence is a "real presence," but a presence better understood in the language of sign (transsignification) than in the language of substance (transsubstantiation). If our God is a bodily God, then he must at all times remain a body. Just as we cannot be present to another under the species of bread and wine, neither can God in any literal sense; if he could, then we would not have a God who shared our humanity. Thus we can only talk of God's presence as that of a presence to us by means of a material sign. The substance of bread and wine remains that of Christ's bodily presence by means of the signs he chose to symbolize that presence. In this sense, he is as fully present to us as a sign as he was once thought to be as a substance.

## III. DEWART

The doctrine of transubstantiation makes a great deal of sense if, but only if, it is first supposed that (a) the basic and most real reality of anything is its substance, and (b) substance is really distinct from accident. Under these conditions, the real presence of the divinity manifested and bequeathed to us by Jesus is perhaps best conceived as the result of a change in the substance of the bread and wine. But these conditions are not unquestionable. In fact, they are no longer connatural to ordinary human experience, and hence it is difficult to believe in the transubstantiation. But I stress that what is difficult is not to believe in *wondrous* metaphysical events: it is to believe in any sort of *metaphysical* events.

If anything in being can be said to have a basic reality other than that which it exercises in the manifestation of its existence, it is not something which underlies this manifestation, but the relation that it has to consciousness—in other words, its meaning. Thus, to say that, although the appearances of bread and wine have not changed, their most basic reality has changed, is to say that the appearances *mean* something different than what they previously meant. In this sense, therefore, they no longer manifest themselves: they manifest something else, namely, the real presence of God among believers. This does not give the eucharist a purely symbolic meaning, if by *symbolic* is meant the same as *metaphorical* or figurative—that is, if *symbolic* is contrasted with *real*. Of course, this *does* give it a symbolic meaning if we remember that a symbol, in the most proper use of the term, is anything in which man embodies his relation to a certain reality. (For instance, is not the Creed, aptly called "The Symbol of the Apostles"?).

But perhaps more important than speculation on the philosophy of the real presence may be the development of its meaning and function in the believer's life. Recent changes in the eucharistic liturgy are encouraging—mostly because they are probably but a token of a process which is leading us to novel and plural forms the final pattern of which cannot be yet foretold. One possibility to be kept in mind is the re-insertion of the eucharist within the larger context of a more or less festive meal. The more significant and indeed more solemn occasions provided by such a practice would imply, of course, a reduction in their frequency. This would serve to enhance the ritual value of the sacrament. No public function which takes place every seven days, fifty-two weeks a year, can fail to become commonplace and routine. And the compulsory character of periodic attendance at Mass could be profitably discontinued immediately, even before constructive reforms take place.

## IV. FRANCIS

I believe that at consecration the substance of the bread and wine at Mass becomes the substance of the Body and Blood of Christ. No ifs, ands, buts, I believe it.

I can understand why this gives some people problems. It gave problems back in the days when Our Lord walked on earth. Some turned away from Him and no longer walked with Him, the Scriptures tell us, because this was too hard a saying.

What do I think substance means? Well, I'll not go into any involved philosophical discussion about it. What I believe is that the substance of something is the deepest truth about it, what it really is in the fullest understanding.

So what was in its fullest meaning only bread and wine is, after consecration, in its deepest meaning, in its fullest truth, the Body and Blood of Christ. It gives me no trouble that a chemical analysis would show the physical properties of bread and wine remained —what does that have to do with the deepest meaning of something?

I also have no trouble with alternate theological teachings. Consubstantiation? Something can not in deepest truth be two entirely different things. Transignification? It strikes me as an attempt to soften a hard saying. Our Lord didn't tell them they would be receiving something that signified His Body. To suggest that only the significance of the bread and wine has changed sounds like the sort of an adjusment in teaching someone would make who was a little embarrassed by hard sayings.

It was Flannery O'Connor, I think, who said that if the Eucharist was only a symbol she'd say to hell with it. Well, it isn't only a symbol. It is one of those hard Christian beliefs that we must accept. Obviously it is an embarrassment to some people, it was when Our Lord first spoke about it. Who would think it wouldn't be now, too.

## V. MATT

Today, when the ancient doctrines on the Holy Eucharist are again under attack, even as in the days when Luther and Zwingli turned the serenity and peace of the Last Supper into a raging controversy over the Real Presence—we Catholics need not be confused or dismayed by the newly evolving controversy concerning this matter. After all, we do have the authoritative teaching of the Church to guide us, today as always, and it is to that infallible teaching that we must turn when conflicting voices begin to be heard.

The opening paragraph of Chapter II of the Constitution on the Sacred Liturgy (Vatican II) reiterates, in outline form, the Church's traditional teaching concerning what it calls the "most sacred mystery of the Eucharist." It tells us this: "At the Last Supper, on the night when He was betrayed, our Savior instituted the Eucharistic Sacrifice of His Body and Blood. He did this in order to perpetuate the Sacrifice of the Cross throughout the centuries until He should come again, and so to entrust to His beloved spouse, the Church, a memorial of His death and resurrection . . ."

The documents of Vatican II are unmistakably clear in this matter as in others. There is no slightest hint in these official pronouncements that the Church has in any sense deviated from her steadfast insistence on the Mass as a Sacrifice rather than a mere Communal Meal, or from its long established doctrine on the Real Presence of Christ in the Holy Eucharist.

Moreover, our present Pontiff, Pope Paul VI, in his splendid encyclical letter *Mysterium Fidei*, makes it abundantly clear that those modern-day Catholics who would in any sense question or even deny the Real Presence of the Body and Blood, Soul and Divinity of Christ in the most Holy Eucharist, or who would substitute such long discredited theories as "transignification" for the doctrinally defined and established teaching of Transubstantiation, are definitely in error. In the face of Neo-Modernists and Rationalists, who incline to give a merely natural explanation to this all-important teaching, the Pontiff once again underscores the exalted "mystery" of the Holy Eucharist and the words of consecration, pointing out that it is the Church alone, the pillar and ground of truth, that guarantees to her children, by her infallible teaching authority, the full and unadulterated revelation of Almighty God. Consequently, it is the first duty of the Faithful to adhere to what the Church proposes as "the proximate norm of faith," which, in reference to the Eucharist, has been infallibly set forth for all time in Sessions XIII, XXI, and XXII of the Council of Trent. The quintessence of these doctrinal, Tridentine decisions consists in this: That in the Eucharist the Body and Blood of the God-man are truly, really, and substantially present for the nourishment of our souls, by reason of the Transubstantiation of the bread and wine into the Body and Blood of Christ, and that, in this change of substances, the unbloody Sacrifice of the New Testament is also contained.

Those, therefore, who either deny outright the literal words used by Christ when He instituted the Eucharistic Sacrifice at the Last Supper, or who would interpret these words in a merely symbolical or figurative sense, are simply repeating the manifold errors of the 16th century "reformers" who, in other respects, too —e.g., by their insistence on a table instead of an altar—emphasized their rejection of the Mass as a Sacrifice and interpreted the words of consecration as a mere symbol. Their various arbitrary theories and contentions, however, were conclusively refuted and condemned by the Church, more specifically by the Council of Trent, whose infallible pronouncements on the matter are still the unwavering position of the Church today.

As for those Catholics in our day who again incline to substitute the Holy Eucharist or Banquet for the Sacrament of Penance or private confession, it is still the authoritative teaching of the Church that anyone in mortal sin cannot receive this Heavenly Bread with profit since, as the Council of Trent explained it, the "chief fruit of the Eucharist does not consist in the forgiveness of sins." For although Christ said of the Chalice: "This is my blood of the new testament, which shall be shed for many unto remission of sins," He had in view *an effect of the sacrifice,* not of the sacrament; for He did not say that His Blood would be *drunk* unto remission of sins, but *shed* for that purpose. It is for this very reason, in fact, that St. Paul demands, as a prerequisite for reception of the Sacrament, a rigorous-self-examination," in order to avoid the heinous offence of being guilty of the Body and Blood of the Lord by "eating and drinking unworthily," and that the Fathers of the Church so emphatically insist upon a pure and innocent conscience as a prerequisite for the reception of the sacrament.

Holy Communion, therefore, must never be considered a substitute for the Sacrament of Penance nor a substitute for Christ's sacrifice and ours.

## VI. SHEED

Christ's presence in the Eucharist is utterly mysterious, nothing in human experience is like it, the mind can be tantalized by it, seeking for ways to explain it. Transubstantiation was one such way, rich in itself, and in its suggestion of further depths. But it did not answer every question, and it was born of a philosophy not congenial to many modern thinkers. Other ways were sought —in particular analyzings of the word "presence," some of them coming close to a symbolical presence, *as if* Christ were present, giving a meaning of the word "real" which did not seem to accord with any meaning of reality known to men.

But "Real Presence" is not a Scriptural phrase. What Christ said was "This is my body." "This is the chalice of my blood." Within a few hours of his death he was not likely to sit there playing with figures of speech which would mislead the vast majority of his followers for 1900 years. They have believed—and I with them—that what he held *was* his body, no longer bread therefore; what was in the cup *was* his blood, not wine. So Paul says notably in 1 Corinthians XI: "He who eats and drinks unworthily will be guilty of profaning the body and the blood of the Lord" —surely an incredible thing to say of a symbol, to say of any presence but what Christians have always called "real."

There are those who say that the Eucharist was given as food and not for adoration. This is to make an unnatural division between what the food is and what it does. He who comes upon the altar for our nourishment *is* adorable, and it would be highly artificial to act as if we did not know this. To quote myself: "Christ in the Host does not become less nourishing by being adored, and the act of adoration has its own way of nourishing the human spirit. . . . Whatever the reason for introducing the Elevation into the Mass, it has splendidly justified itself. Who would wish to forego the moment when we join together in adoring him whom we are individually to receive?"

*How* Christ can be "wholly and entirely present" we do not know, but for the *fact* we have Christ's word. *Fact* of course is more important than *how*: yet we do long for more light. And Vatican II looks for further explanation of the Mystery to "arrive at greater clarity, greater accuracy."

# 13. WHAT MUST A MAN DO
## TO BE SAVED?

## I. BUCKLEY

I think a man in order to be saved has to make conscious efforts
to be at least a little bit better than his sluggish moral nature
would end him up being. I don't know what the objective standards are and I don't think it is really exactly specified, but can't
we all agree that it does require people at certain critical points
in their life to say I am going to do such and such, not because
it is my bent to do such and such, but because such and such is
the right thing to do. I don't adopt the Pelagian position that we
have total sovereignty over our own salvation. I adopt the more
orthodox position that if we desire to be saved, we will be granted
the grace of fortitude but that we have to contribute to the
cooperation with that grace.

## II. CALLAHAN

This question presupposes that man is somehow lost. I do not
accept that presupposition. Man stands in need of fulfillment and
in need of escaping those limitations which make him prone to
evil and sin. But these things he can only achieve himself. He
cannot be saved by another; that is, he cannot be fulfilled by
another. If he is to fulfill himself, then he must learn to love
himself and to love his neighbor. In the person of Christ, we have
the gift of seeing what self-love and love of neighbor means.
Faith in the person of Christ does not save us; what does save us
is faith that we can be like, and be one with, Christ. Some do not

have the gift of Christ, at least not consciously. But they do have the gift of their own potentialities for love. Insofar as they are able to realize these potentialities will they be fulfilled—will they become one with themselves and with others. Should they come to know Christ, they will come to see with their own eyes the fullest meaning of love. But even if they do not come to know Christ, they can come to perceive the meaning of love. That Christ once lived among us means that he continues to exist in the minds of men as an exemplar of love, as the very embodiment of love. In the Eucharist, he lives on as an efficacious sign that the love he embodied has not left this earth. That is a sign which proclaims itself to all men. That is a sign which means that embodied love remains with us; but it is not the only sign—the Church is another, so are our fellow Christians individually.

## III. DEWART

This is, of course, the basic question underlying every religious enquiry. If the answer were simple or clear religious reflection could safely cease.

Perhaps the beginning of wisdom is indeed the thought that this is not an easy question—above all because the problem is not simply that of finding a presently unavailable (or an elusive) means to attain an otherwise clearly delimited and obviously all-valuable end. The problem is almost precisely the opposite. For we may be reasonably certain that, whatever may be that to which we ought to direct ourselves—I mean, with an ultimate self-commitment—the means to achieve it can be, in general, no other than the exercise of our free, creative existence in the presence of God. The problem is that it is not so very easy to determine what, in concrete, we must undertake as the central and final project of our total life. Nor must we suppose that this project must be the same for everyone: to each life of creative freedom corresponds a vocation (which is itself subject to evolution throughout life) which is not clearly definable except to the very degree that it is undertaken in faith, hope and love.

Evidently, then, "salvation" is not so much a question of finding out in what may consist one's ultimate "safety," one's ultimate rescue from an inhospitable situation. It is rather (if I may be forgiven a capitalist, but instructive, metaphor) a question of finding out what constitutes a wise investment of one's free existence. The traditional metaphor, "salvation," has become most unhelpful—perhaps it has become even a positive moral hindrance—because it has been applicable only at that level of human development when man naturally and understandably perceived his situation within reality as fraught with dangers beyond his control. This is not so nearly true today—at least not in the more advanced cultures—when the danger of the human situation comes not so much from external forces of nature as from the evil possibilities inherent in man. The dangers we need fear today are not hunger, pestilence, disease and abject ignorance: they are self-destruction, genocide, cultural demoralization, institutionalized anarchy and self-induced hallucinations on a national if not global scale. Perhaps, then, the question is better put today in other terms than "salvation." How can man find ultimate meaning in conscious existence freely undertaken? How can I best discharge the final and total responsibility in which I am placed by the fact of being conscious that I exist? In what way should I definitively orient myself, keeping in mind that the definitiveness of human temporality is given by the termination of life in death?

We should remember, moreover, that although creative speculation about these problems is most valuable (and it is a pity that Catholic thought has so long neglected it, having been excessively occupied with other, largely archaeological, tasks), the questions themselves are not speculative. No answer to them is adequate unless it be in some sense worked out by oneself, and unless it be worked out above all in and through one's conscious life and freely exercised existence.

## IV. Francis

I think that I can best express my position by stating that I believe no man is condemned to hell except that he deliberately choose to disobey what he knows God asks of him.

Therefore, I would believe all those who do the will of God as they know the will of God will be saved.

A man either turns towards God or away from God. Here is a man of good will. He knows little or nothing about God and his ignorance is not culpable for nothing in his ordinary life leads him to fuller knowledge. But he acts according to those standards he believes to be right, wanting to do right. He dies in this state, without baptism, without any Christian commitment. I would believe he would be saved. God extends lines. The line of life that moves in his direction even when it is ended is extended by God and the man is saved.

Another man might be a nominal Christian. He may fulfill of the stated requirements, baptism, membership, faithful attendance at Mass. But he had hatred for people who do not look, act or think exactly as he does. He has no concern for others, his sole concern is for himself. He dies leaving his estate to the Church but I would think it might very well be difficult for him to save his soul if he died in an attitude of hatred towards other people and with no compassion on them for their needs.

## V. MATT

Keep the commandments, of course. But in order to keep God's commandments man must first learn to know, love and serve God, both as individuals and as members of Christ's Mystical Body, so that the Divine Redeemer of mankind, "who has become for us God-given wisdom, and justice, and sanctification, and redemption" (1 Cor 1:30) may rule the hearts of men and nations, ordering all things and restoring tranquillity and peace to a world that is gravely ill. In one of the decrees of the Second Vatican Council we are told that "whoever follows after Christ, the perfect Man, becomes himself more of a man" (*Const. on the Chuch in the Modern World*). This practical following of Christ can only mean that we, as citizens of two cities, must strive to discharge our responsibilities faithfully and well, both to God and to Caesar, penetrating the world with the true Christian spirit and seeing to it, as the Council puts it, "that the divine law is inscribed in the life of the earthly city." But the key to this conscientious living of the Christ life, as Vatican II so aptly states, is filial obedience, the same exemplary obedience practiced by Christ Himself "who by His obedience even unto death, opened to all men the blessed way of the liberty of the children of God" (*Const. on the Church*, chap. 37). In order, therefore, not only to be saved but to demonstrate our gratitude for this hoped-for salvation by God, we must learn to love God above all things and our neighbor *because of God*. Indeed, in order that this love—so often poorly defined nowadays!—brings forth good fruit in our own souls and in the souls of others, we must not only *hear* the Word of God and accept His holy will in all things, but we must strive to *complete* what God has already begun in us by His redemptive act, when He reconciled us to His heavenly Father and gave us a share in His redemptive mission of saving and sanctifying immortal souls. The Christian is called, therefore, not only to save his own soul but to help restore sanity and sanctity to a dangerously disordered and sick society!

But in order to do this, it is necessary that religion again begin to address itself to questions of ultimate concern rather than to social-political questions. Indeed, as the well-known liberal rabbi, Arthur Hertzberg, of Temple Emanu-El in Englewood, N.J., observed recently, the "nervous scurrying for relevance" by politically active clergymen may represent the sickness, not the health, of American religion today. (*N.Y. Times*, March 10). Rabbi Hertzberg finds "a large part of what passes for liberal religion in America today as a rewriting of *The Nation* and *The New Republic*." He thinks "that's not the job of religion," which should be concerned instead with ultimate metaphysical truths, for which people are hungering. Rabbi Hertzberg believes that Christians who are currently trying to revitalize their religion by making it socially relevant should note the experience of Jews, who started doing the same thing a century ago. "Having been there for a hundred years and played the game," he says, "I can tell you that it doesn't work. The very moment that clerics become more worldly, the world goes to hell all the faster." Believers can and should become involved in social questions, he maintains, but they must not deceive themselves into thinking that this is religious leadership, or that they are doing anything more than tagging onto the end of a secular culture. The role of religion, according to the Rabbi, is not to gain acceptance in the secular world or "to lend the blessing of the church or synagogue to a popular front." People nowadays, he insists, "are not very happy" with such antics on our part. "They are worried about something more than Dow Chemical and napalm. They are worried about what's it all for. They are worried about—dare I say it?—immortality, what their lives are linked to." He suggests—and in this I heartily concur with the Rabbi—that the chief energies of clergymen should be devoted to discussing the existence of God and man's obedience to God, rather than to political issues. "Liberal religion is faintly out of date," he declares. "We are moving past the social question to questions of ultimate concern." What must be done if men are to save their own souls and the souls of others is to put religion back on the right track, i.e., let its chief concern be "love and God and the transcendant," rather than the worn-out preachments of socio-political revolution.—Amen!

## VI. Sheed

Saved from what? "You shall call his name Jesus because he will save his people from their sins." He offers us salvation not from our enemies or our sufferings, but our sins: that is, from ourselves. Sin is the thrust of self towards what we want, away from what God wants, our will set against God's will. It is a denial of love, a turning from life, these being inseparable—diminish either and we diminish the other, grow in either and we grow in the other. Sin is what Christ came to save us from, life is what he came to save us to, life here, life hereafter. We cannot be saved without him, but we cannot be saved without ourselves either.

What must we *do* to be saved? His answer lists two kinds of doing and one of receiving.

To the question "What must I do to inherit eternal life," he answered "Keep the commandments—do not kill, do not commit adultery. . . ." (Mk 10:19). The commandments are our Maker's statement of the right way to handle ourselves; keeping them is the way to health, to life. But he adds two, written in the Old Testament but not in the Ten, as vitalizing the rest—Love God with every element of your being; love your neighbor as yourself: "On these depend the law and the prophets" (Mk 11:31). Sin is the refusal of love, our self loved to the exclusion of God and fellow-men. To observe the Decalogue to the letter without love is not the way to inherit eternal life. (Paul writes a rhapsody on this 1 Corinthians 13). Love and commandments require each other, "If you love me, keep my commandments" (Jn 14:15).

Love of neighbor issues in the second thing he tells us we are to do to be saved—feed the hungry and the thirsty, clothe the naked, visit the sick (Mt 25)—failure in these constitutes Christ's answer to the question nobody ever asked him—What must a man do to be damned?

Love and life, we note, are inseparable, and life too figures in his answer to our question. "Unless a man be born again"—unless that is he enters into another dimension of life—"he will not enter the Kingdom of God" (Jn 3:5). And "unless you shall eat the flesh of the Son of Man and drink his blood you shall not have life in you (Jn 6:54).

But, as Augustine reminds us, we are bound by the sacraments, God is not. Upon our salvation, what we love will be decisive.

# 14. FREEDOM OF CONSCIENCE VIS À VIS CHURCH AUTHORITY

## I. BUCKLEY

The current problem has to do with the enlargement of the operative role of conscience, and this is the result of the prevailing narcissism. We tend so to diminish the role of authority that we go wantonly the way of the conscience and in doing so neglect to apply those sutures on the conscience that St. Thomas advises to apply. It seems to me that the Church has an obligation to especially emphasize the fact that to follow one's conscience without a total consultation and a submissive consultation with the contending position as specified by the Church is an act of hubris, and as such something that tends ultimately to distinguish the pagan rather than the Christian.

One has to recognize that those people who speak so confidently about the supremacy of the conscience haven't really faced up to the consequences of that supremacy. For instance, it is altogether possible that the person who shot down Martin Luther King thought of himself as acting in total correspondence with the dictates of his conscience. I don't think that people who preach supremacy of conscience would be happy in a world in which everybody pursued only the dictates of his conscience. It would be sort of a Randite world, a world in which all of the leavening of Christianity has vanished. Somebody, hell, everybody, has remarked that probably more damage has been done in the world by people who intend to do good than by people who intend to commit evil.

## II. CALLAHAN

The human conscience is always free in the face of Church authority. It has the obligation of listening to authority, of taking it seriously, and of trying to respect it. But the human conscience can not hand itself over to Church authority, or ever allow it to make a decision for us. Human beings are responsible for their own lives; to abrogate this responsibility in favor of Church authority is to abnegate one's very humanity; and this is morally intolerable. Whatever authority may claim for itself—and its claims have traditionally been pretentious—human beings have the obligation of judging that authority, of sifting and weighing its claims. Where these claims infringe upon the conscience, they must be rejected. The teaching authority of the Catholic Church has not distinguished itself over the centuries. Its biblical and juridical claims to teach in the name of the Lord would have been much more plausible if it had displayed an ability to teach with charismatic and moral authority. This it has rarely been able to do. That the magisterium is forced to rely so heavily upon the purported and dubious biblical and traditional basis of its power is testimony to the weakness of its prima facie moral authority. If, in the years ahead, the magisterium is able to demonstrate its moral authority, I will quite gladly reconsider my presently negative evaluation of its legal claims.

## III. DEWART

It is difficult to say something sensible on this point which has not already been said by John L. MacKenzie. I will merely suggest here that much misunderstanding concerning the nature of freedom of conscience stems from a prior misunderstanding of the nature of freedom. Freedom is not the absence of necessitation of man's will: it is the pro-spective, pro-jective dimension, the future-tensional orientation of man's conscious, intelligent existence. Thus, if one is human, one *cannot* fail to exercise one's freedom. We are not free to decide whether or not we are free: we are *already* free. But we can either freely accept our freedom or we can freely abdicate it. Of course, even our decision to abdicate our freedom is a free decision by which we project ourselves towards the future. Likewise, the inner contradiction involved in the abdication of one's conscience reveals it as a misuse of freedom. Freedom of conscience, therefore, is not an inalienable personal right of the individual; it is the quality of the human existent as responsible for his personal creation.

It follows that the religious relations between man and God and, *a fortiori*, those of the believer and ecclesiastical authorities, are not adequately conceived in terms of the competing claims between the will of the one and the authority of the (divine or ecclesiastical) other. It may be more adequate to think of them in terms of distinct, albeit complementary, responsibilities. The individual is to God or to ecclesiastical authority, as responsibility is to challenge. Conversely, the supremacy of God and the legitimate authority of ecclesiastical rulers are not to be understood as demands for submission—not even as reasonable and benevolent demands for submission. They may be better understood as forms of self-communication the characteristic of which is that they challenge and stimulate.

## IV. FRANCIS

That there is a primacy of the conscience seems to me certain. The question is where you exercise this primacy. My acceptance of the Church as the Church of Jesus Christ leads me—and this itself is an act of my conscience—to accept the magisterium of the Church. On a different level, my acceptance of my responsibilities as a citizen of the United States leads me to accept the laws and regulations of the society of which I am a member.

But if there would be a conflict with my conscience in a particular instance, either on the level of my membership in the Mystical Body of Christ or on the level of my membership in the secular society, I would not hesitate to follow the dictates of my conscience.

But as a member of the Church my ordinary course would be to accept the magisterium of the Church and my resort to private conscience would be to a court of last resort, only when I was absolutely certain that to obey the magisterium of the Church would surely be a violation of my personal conscience.

The difficulty today is that too many are making their personal consciences the point of first encounter. In doing this they are cutting themselves off from not only the wisdom of the past but the guidance the Holy Spirit offers the whole Church.

## V. MATT

Despite everything written and said on this subject these past few years, there is, as I see it, nothing essentially new to be said. Those of us who are now middle-aged and beyond remember well from our childhood training the teaching of the Church with respect to one's personal conscience, i.e., we must obey our lawful superiors, including in first place our parents, as the representatives of God Himself, in all things, that is, except sin. Even our parents, we were told, cannot expect our obedience in the event that they asked us to defy God's law and commit sin. Of course, we are sometimes tempted to believe that our personal human rights would be more genuinely served if we were exempted from every requirement even of Divine Law. But, as the Second Vatican Council explicitly reminds us, in "this way lies not the maintenance of the dignity of the human person, but its annihilation." (*Const. on the Church in the Modern World*, para. 41, p. 39).

Those, therefore, who nowadays champion such things as "holy disobedience" where the institutional Church is concerned appear to be on shaky ground. Pope Paul VI, in his encyclical *Ecclesiam Suam*, makes abundantly clear that faithful obedience to Christ and His Church is a foremost virtue and quite indispensable. The Church, he declares, "will rediscover her renewed youthfulness not so much by changing her exterior laws as by interiorly assimilating her true spirit of obedience to Christ and, accordingly, by observing those laws which the Church prescribes for herself with the intention of following Christ." Church law, he writes, today as always "retains its essential binding force" and the true Christian life "will always require faithfulness, effort, mortification and sacrifice." It will require "not less moral energy of us modern

Christians than it did of Christians in the past, but perhaps more. It will call for a prompt obedience, no less binding today than in the past." The same Pontiff's words (para. 53) are, I feel, eminently worth repeating here: "It is not conformity with the spirit of the world, not immunity from the discipline of reasonable asceticism, not indifference to the laxity of modern behavior, not emancipation from the authority of prudent and lawful superiors, not apathy with regard to the contradictory forms of modern thought that can give vigor to the Church or render her following of Christ more genuine . . . (Rather) the hierarchic constitution of the Church requires (para. 118) that, on the one side, authority should be exercized according to its proper function and that, on the other side, there should be submission . . . i.e., the observance of canonical regulations and respect for the government of legitimate superiors in the spirit of untroubled readiness as becomes free and loving children." "The spirit of independence, of criticism, of rebellion ill accords with the charity which gives life to the Church's solidarity, concord and peace, and easily transfers the dialogue into argument, dispute and disagreement."

*Authority, hierarchy, obedience*—these things are stressed over and over again in the official constitutions and decrees of Vatican II. I would suggest, therefore, for those Catholics who still believe that an ecumenical council is always presided over by the Divine Paraclete, the Spirit of Truth, that they heed this Spirit and submit to His infallible prescriptions in this and in related matters.

## VI. SHEED

What is conscience? An inner voice, we say. But whose voice? Our own. It is a decision we ourselves make as to the moral rightness of some action done, or to be done, by ourselves. We are bound to follow it, yet it is no more certainly right than any other decision we make. Over the world and through the centuries we find conscience universal, but its judgments immeasurably various, abominations often enough approved by it. Precisely because we are bound to follow conscience, we must take every means of ensuring that its judgments are right.

For the Catholic the Church's teaching is such a means—by

Christ's commission she is to teach men to observe all things what-soever he has commanded. This does not mean setting up the Church as a rival to conscience. If we accept the Church, then her teaching is one of the elements by which our mind forms the judgment which is our conscience.

If all commands came to us direct from God, conscience would present no problem (though acting in accordance with it still would). For the most part his will is clear—Christ's moral teaching as recorded in the Gospels is much easier to be certain about than His doctrinal teaching. But not all the Church's teaching on right and wrong in human conduct claims infallibility—some of it is her own application to human life of the unchanging principles God has entrusted to her.

Problems arise when a man finds a conflict between the Church's application and his own conscience. The command is not infallible but neither is his conscience. Weighing a fallible utterance of the Church against a fallible utterance of his conscience, he might decide that the judgment of the bishops is more likely to be right than his own—if so his conscience judges for acceptance. But if his conscience is certain that he cannot accept, it is his conscience that he must follow.

As things are now, this means being barred from the sacraments. This could mean anguish. It would not be a reason for leaving the Church, which is still Christ's even if its officials have acted wrongly. If the Catholic maintains his love for the men who have barred him, then he is suffering not only for his belief but for the Church and his suffering works for its renewal.

# 15. THE ROLE OF CATHOLIC SCHOOLS

## I. BUCKLEY

The Catholic schools do have a role provided they maintain their Catholicity conspicuously enough to warrant their maintenance as separate institutions, otherwise why have them. I sympathize with any criticism of any Catholic school that says "look, the standards aren't high enough intellectually, but go ahead and repair those standards as you can," but I say at the same time let's make it what it needs to be, namely, an experience that always suggests the spiritual dimension of all life. How to do that is simply something that tests the pedagogical and imaginative skills of the administration. But I am thoroughly out of sympathy with those who simply take the position in effect that there ought to be no really observable difference between a Catholic school and a non-Catholic school, other than perhaps a quaint little chapel on the premises.

## II. CALLAHAN

In the light of my undoubtedly heretical views on a number of other issues of more fundamental theological significance, it may come as a surprise that I am increasingly favorable toward Catholic schools. A very bad Catholic school seems to me a terrible thing to wish upon a child, but a very good Catholic school can be of great value. In a pluralistic society, it seems to me particularly useful to have schools which prepare people in significantly different ways than the public schools; too few Catholic schools actually do this, but they should. I have had enough experience with the public school system, and the conformist power of a secular culture as it expresses itself in that system, to convince me that most anti-school liberal Catholics have an illusory view of the possibility of children withstanding the bad features of that system and the culture it represents. At the same time, most of my own experiences, and that of many friends, with the Catholic schools suggest that it is equally illusory to think that they do much better than the public schools. That leaves me, then, with a dilemma: what does one do when neither alternative seems very good? My own solution would be to strengthen the Catholic schools. That seems to me far more possible than to strengthen the public schools (which is not to say one shouldn't try). I should also add, though, that I think there are many more important ways to spend our money than on the Catholic schools. If there were an infinite amount of money, I would try to make the schools better. But there isn't, and the money should probably be spent in other ways (on the poor, slums, etc.). Though I would myself make this latter choice, I would do so unhappily since, in principle, I see much hope for a good Catholic school system, from primary to college level.

## III. DEWART

What one thinks of the appropriateness of Catholic schools should reflect above all what one thinks about education. Frequently, however, it really reflects mostly what one thinks about the Church. Part of the reason is, no doubt, that the term "Catholic education" does not actually mean simply what it says, "education insofar as it is affected by the Catholic faith." It means rather "education controlled by the hierarchy or clerical congregations."

To the latter sort of educational arrangements there may well be valid objections at specific times and places. But to the idea of Catholic education properly so-called there should be none— provided that the educational institutions fulfill in the first place their function as educational, and that their Catholicity should be superadded to them.

In the practical order this approach to Catholic education would mean, for instance, that the resources of the Catholic community should be so allotted as to give priority to the provision of a Catholic dimension at the higher levels of education, and to quality rather than to quantity. A single, good, research-oriented, pace-setting Catholic university is worth to the Catholic community more than a large number of mediocre ones, or than an even larger number of parish-run elementary schools. This assumes, of course, that the value of Catholic educational institutions does not lie in the number of souls it (supposedly) helps "save," but in the contribution it can make to the development of the collective Catholic intellect.

## IV. FRANCIS

I believe in Catholic education. I am a product of public schools and my knowledge of Catholic schools comes second hand through my children. I believe that Catholic schools match public schools in quality and add another dimension that public schools cannot add in our pluralistic society.

I would not be satisfied with the quality of Catholic schools, nor would I be satisfied with the quality of public schools. We should certainly seek excellence in all education.

I do not believe Catholic schools are a divisive factor in the secular society. My own particular experience has demonstrated to me that Catholic parochial schools—at least in the smaller cities—manage to cut across social stratas better than the traditional public neighborhood schools.

I believe it is important to establish the primacy of parental rights in choice of schools. Public schools exist as a means for implementing parental choice of education, so do parochial schools. Since both exist identically as secondary means for fulfillment of primary parental rights, it seems to me that both should be supported equally by the taxes provided for education.

The best means to achieve this could come through providing something not unlike the educational provisions of the G.I. Bill. Public agencies would set certain basic standards. Those schools that met these standards would be accredited. Funds would be set aside, both federal, state and local, and where the pupil went would go whatever funds established for his educational costs. I believe this is both constitutional and equitable.

The alternative is, I fear, a monolithic educational system under state domination in which parochial school education would be destroyed for all except the affluent, able to pay rising taxes for state schools and for parochial tuition. This, I believe, would be harmful for the nation.

## V. MATT

While the Second Vatican Council has reaffirmed the Church's teaching on the role of the Catholic school and of the parents' anterior rights and duties governing the formation of their off-spring, the fact remains that gradually but nonetheless inexorably the Catholic schools, at least in our own country, are being phased out of existence not merely for lack of funds and teaching personnel but for want of those ancient, rock-ribbed Catholic convictions and absolute ideals that once animated our forebears in the founding and furtherance of these same schools. In contradistinction to the permissive, progressivist, secularist atmosphere pervading most of our present-day schools, our Catholic school administrators of bygone days understood in first place the nature of the *subject* of education, namely, man—including his congenital weaknesses and disordered inclinations as a consequence of Original Sin. Hence they sought in first place to *correct* in the students these disordered tendencies and to *strengthen* their moral fibre, by stressing supernatural, metaphysical truth, and by emphasizing the importance of the sacraments and the life of grace in individual souls. Hence, by and large, they steered clear of what Pius XI called those diverse forms of "pedagogic naturalism (including so-called Sex Education!) which exclude or weaken supernatural Christian formation in the teaching of youth" and which cater to "a pretended self-government and unrestrained freedom on the part of the child," attributing to him an "exclusive primacy of initiative and an activity independent of any higher law, natural or divine." (*Encyclical on Christian Education*) To the extent that our Catholic schools have digressed from the basic principles set forth in the above encyclical written in 1929, to that extent it appears to me our schools have forfeited their very reason for existence and are perhaps doomed, as Pius XI warned, not only to fail of their purpose but to "become instead an agent of destruction."

## VI. McLuhan

The role of Catholic schools naturally differs from one culture to another. In Nigeria or among the Eskimos Catholic education means what it did in ancient Gaul—the bringing of literacy and civilization to a tribal world. In the electric age, telegraph, radio and television are re-tribalizing the most advanced literate societies at much higher speeds than the process of literacy was ever applied to tribal societies. De-tribalization simply means the substituting of the highly specialist visual world for the very inclusive and unified world of oral cultures. That Catholic education should from its early days have been identified with the infusion of a Graeco-Roman technology and outlook is a matter that needs much attention in the present age. Today the area of education that remains within the literary orbit of Graeco-Roman civilization is diminishing very rapidly. The entire Western world through electric technology is in the process of abandoning its entire visual heritage. Electricity as used for information movement and the creation of new environments is a direct extension of our central nervous system. Literary culture at no time ever had any such dimension of human involvement. Visual and literary education fostered the habit of the outer trip and outer exploration. The Oriental world in common with all tribal societies has fostered the inner trip of meditation in depth. Such is also the bent and bias of our new electronic technology. The orientalization of the Western world is far advanced. Civilization, a form of perception and organization based entirely on the phonetic alphabet, is in a state of rapid and universal decline. The time may not be far off when a need to study the Scriptures may be a solitary link between culture and Graeco-Roman literacy. In such an event what would be the role of Catholic schools?

Perhaps it is a mistake to think of Catholic schools in terms of the curriculum at all. As the world environment becomes increasingly programmed into a universal teaching machine, Catholic schools as places to acquire instruction suited to use in the outer world, would become quite useless. Throughout His Ministry, Our Lord was very equivocal about literacy. "It is written, but I say unto you." The scribes and the Pharisees, the Jewish establishment, got very low marks from Him: "Faith comes by hearing."

School is from *scholia*, meaning "leisure," and leisure is total involvement. The artist never works. He is always at leisure because he always uses all his faculties. Specialism, the ignoble condition of using only part of one's powers has always been associated with the idea of servitude. In the electric age when the environment itself become a teaching machine, every moment of existence can be one of enrichment and enlightenment. It is such an environment that the universal abundance of divine grace provides in perpetuity. It is the specialist who deprives himself of access to this environment. If the Catholic schools of the future choose to program themselves electrically they could create a symmetry between the secular environment of information and the environment of grace. A school as a place of subjects and credit would become obsolescent, as indeed it is strongly tending to do. The problems, therefore, of programming Catholic education are likely to become many times greater than at any time in the history of the Church.

## VII. SHEED

With the State providing a complete school system, the only justification for separate Catholic schools is that they give something essential in the field of Education which the State cannot give.

Education, as a minimum, means fitting human beings for

living. This involves, again as a minimum, knowing what the purpose of life is. And this the State as State does not know.

Any citizen is free to answer the question in any one of a dozen ways according to his Religion or agnosticism or atheism, and the State is not allowed by law to decide among them.

The Catholic feels that what God has revealed through Christ as to the goal of life and how the goal is to be reached is relevant to fitting men for living, that any system which omits it is educationally defective, based solely upon the fragment of reality which lies between conception and death. The function of the Catholic school is to teach what is necessary for life on this earth in the framework of Christ's revelation of life as a whole—all things related to God and so to each other.

How far has the Catholic school fulfilled this function? Not invariably well. Until very recently the teaching of religion was really bad, being too often entrusted to teachers who would not have been allowed to teach any other subject of which they knew so little. Even where the teachers have a sound knowledge of theology, there has been a failure to make Christ central. A phenomenon long noted has been a falling away from Mass and sacraments once school days were over; it has quite suddenly grown to a frightening size, a real evaporation of Faith, Christ evaporating with the rest. And this at a time when schools have become enormously more expensive, with teachers paid more, school-leaving age raised, far more equipment needed. So we face the double question whether the Catholic body can find the money, whether it is worth the money (*and* the time and the effort—all for the young, none left over for the adult Catholic).

Education is still defective, save in the framework of life as a whole which Christ gives. But it is not unthinkable that this might be learned outside school—at home or in Church perhaps —with such knowledge as the State's schools give enriched by it and enriching it.

# 16. CELIBACY OF THE CLERGY

## I. BUCKLEY

I am considered very heterodox in the *Triumph* set because I have never thought of celibacy as other than a socio-psychological decision. It seems to me obvious that there is a dissipation of the moral energies of any human being who has to think simultaneously about his family and his Church and his flock. The idea of being wedded to the Church strikes me as the single most romantic conceivable union. I have nothing but total respect for men who are willing to consummate that union. But I do believe that rather than to ask men who are not diposed to make that unilateral commitment to forego active professional ministry, it would be better to at least make available some priestly orders which married men could join. My notion of what would be ideal is to have priests who elect and those who do not elect celibacy, but let there be both positions.

## II. CALLAHAN

Clerical celibacy should be an entirely optional matter, having no relationship to the office of priest. A priest should have the choice at any time during his priestly career of marrying, with no penalties whatever attached to making that choice. The reasoning of Pope Paul VI in his recent encyclical on celibacy seemed to me wrong at almost every crucial point. However, that said, I would also want to stress the great value of the celibate life for the priest. Its value is strictly a functional one: it does or can free a man to serve in the fullest way possible. As a "sign," especially what has been called an "eschatological sign," celibacy has no value at all; that traditional emphasis should be dropped. Its value is strictly practical, but that is considerable—for some people in some situations (and they are the only ones who should have the right to judge). If there has been any unfortunate consequence of the celibacy discussion, it has been two-fold: 1) That the Pope and the Bishops have so obstinately stuck to a wrongheaded tradition, thus misusing their authority and misusing those priests they should be trying to serve. 2) That the whole discussion has been spoiled by a mystique of marriage which presumes that marriage undoubtedly confers some great liberating personalism and depth on those who are married. Both the married and the celibate state have an equal potential for human relationships; both have an equal potential for selfishness. A decision on celibacy should be made in the light of personal desires, goals and inclinations, not on the basis of the supposed superiority of one state to another. Perfection in human relationships is not something conferred by a basic choice of ways of life, married or celibate, but something achieved by hard work and dedication. I hope that many priests who would be better off married will get married, permission or not. I also hope that many priests who are actually doing quite well as celibates will not let themselves be stampeded into marriage.

## III. DEWART

Whether the clergy should be free to marry is, up to a point, a question for the clergy itself to determine. But the priesthood is, of course, a public office of the Church: the Church's decision on this matter must be ultimately determined by the needs of the Church as a whole. It is regrettable that the recent debate on the subject has been largely conducted (by all sides) as if the matter were formerly the celibacy of the *clergy*, which is a juridical and sociological part of the Church, rather than the celibacy of the *priesthood*, which is a religious office which exists for the sake of the Church as a whole. To be sure, clerkship, as the very etymology of the word indicates, is closely associated with priesthood. Nonetheless, in the Catholic Church they became perfectly distinct long ago.

Now, what is good for the clergy as such is not necessarily good for the priesthood nor, therefore, for the Church. Indeed, there may even exist a certain incompatibility between the two: the declericalization of the priesthood, like any other move in the direction of greater sociological homogeneity within the Church, is by definition detrimental to the clerical status—and yet it may be a great good for the Church. It seems to me that the abolition of the long-established canonical incompatibility between marriage and orders, amounting in practice to granting the priest precisely the same degree of self-determination in relation to marriage as every other member of the Church enjoys, would greatly enhance the priesthood, precisely because it would tend to diminish clericalism in the Church.

The widespread and relatively open discussion of this problem in the Church in recent times—and it would be rash to suppose the final word on the subject has been pronounced—has already had tangible benefits. Celibacy is no longer justified on the supposed value of its strictly negative quality as un-marriage—though it is an open question how prevalent may still be the mysogynist attitudes which in the past have sometimes entered into it. The positive value of celibacy, that the unmarried are free to undertake certain spiritually valuable modes of life which are by nature closed to the married (and, of course, vice versa), shines forth more clearly because the matter has been discussed. However, much confusion remains. To demonstrate that it is fitting and valuable for some Christians to remain celibate for specifically religious reason is not in the least to demonstrate that every priest should be celibate. The opposite assumption is nevertheless frequently made, despite the fact that (at least so far as I can see) it is utterly baseless.

## IV. FRANCIS

Certainly there is nothing in the vocation to the priesthood that requires that the vocation to the priesthood be accompanied by a vocation to the celibate life.

If at a particular time in history, it is believed by those who have the responsibility for the governing of the Church that only those should be ordained to the priesthood who have the vocation to the celibate life then I would believe such a rule could be accepted.

I do not doubt there have been those who have fulfilled their vocation to the priesthood and only endured the vocation to the celibate life. I have compassion for them.

Whether the rule should be changed, I do not know. The Pope, who has held this ruling for himself, has said he believes that celibacy for the Western priesthood should continue. I would accept his decision.

I do not believe that the decline in vocations has any relationship to celibacy; after all there is a decline in vocations to the ministry in Protestantism, too. But then I do not much hold to what some offer as practical arguments for celibacy—that an unmarried priest is freer to fulfill the tasks of his ministry. Again the Protestant experience demonstrates that many clergymen with wives and families give themselves fully to their ministry.

But if the so-called practical arguments do not reach me, there is a beauty in the fullness of the commitment to the celibate life that I do believe has valid meaning. No man should choose the celibate life thinking of it only as a rejection of marriage; it is far more meaningful than this, an affirmation of complete commitment to God that carries with it no sign of negation.

## V. Matt

While Catholic laymen are being admonished over and over again to "renew" themselves spiritually, intellectually, by familiarizing themselves with the Constitutions and Decrees of the Second Vatican Council, it appears that our clergy all too frequently "renew" themselves not by what the Council did or said but by what they *imagine* that Council to have said or by invoking what is loosely described as "the Council's spirit." Were our clergy truly familiar with the Council documents—particularly those on the Priestly Ministry and the Training for the Priesthood —they might have learned by now, as the Council tells them, that "by using to the full every means both human and divine to make their renunciation of marriage so much a part of themselves," they will, instead of impairing their life or work, obtain "greater physical and psychological mastery, the advantage of a greater maturity, and a fuller share of that happiness promised by the Gospel" (*Decree on Training for the Priesthood*). Let our clergy but read and carefully ponder the words of the Council (in the *Decree on the Priestly Ministry and Life*), especially the Chapter on Celibacy (16), and they will realize how important it is to retain celibacy not only as "a symbol and a stimulus to pastoral charity" but as "a unique source of fruitful holiness in the modern world." The Council literally begged not only priests but all of the faithful "to esteem this precious gift of clerical celibacy and to beg God to grant it ever more abundantly to the Church." I wonder: Does it not occur to some of the new breed priests that the more they agitate and whine about their lot as celibates, the more encouragement they give to people in the married state who are weary of the vows they made and are looking for some kind of "new freedom" to release them and license them for greener pastures!

## VI. Sheed

Having seen the Church (and seen it from inside) in more parts of the world than many, having met more priests than most priests have met, having seen just about every fault and failure that priests are supposed to be liable to, I admire the clergy immensely and feel the advantage of their celibacy to us whom they serve.

But do the clergy themselves feel it a greater burden than they should be asked to bear? Only they can know.

# 17. CONTRACEPTION

## I. BUCKLEY

My own intuitive position is not opposed to contraception. I do think that the Pope has done us a disservice by his ambiguity, when one takes into consideration the awful final meaning of any definitive statement. I have, I guess, read more on this subject than I have on other vexed theological questions and I tend to the conclusion that it is not an obvious violation of the marital ideal to permit contraception. I am aware that one has to enter the subject with due deference to all those terribly crucial distinctions—the difference between a contraceptive and an abortifacient for instance. I don't want to go into those details because I don't think you want my views on them but suffice it to say I am aware of those distinctions but I believe that Erik von Kuehnelt Leddihn is convincing and Noonan is convincing in suggesting that the anti-contraception dogma, which is really a lay dogma, grew out of a tendency concerning contraception which was rooted in an anti-Manichaean argument. As I understand it, Noonan's historical observations have to do with the notion that the anti-contraceptive position had something to do with the old idea that fleshly pursuits were unhealthy because they were fleshly and therefore we had to justify the fleshly pursuit of sexual intercourse in terms of procreation.

I am absolutely baffled by people who apparently are unconcerned with the problem of population explosion. I am just absolutely baffled by it. It seems to me that it is obvious that the whole notion of limitation of the size of a family, which notion has been sanctified by the Church, is the microcosm which entitles us to ask macro-cosmic questions. For instance, how large a population can the earth ultimately provide for? To say that it is alright for a family to plan the size of the family with some reference to the resources of that family, sets up what becomes a sorites, on over to what can the community support, what can the region support, what can the continent support, what can the hemisphere support, what can the earth support.

I would side against, emphatically against, any coercive restraints by society. These I would judge to be in clear violation of the natural law over the sovereignty of the individual in deciding how large his family would be. But I would consent, subject to the prior consent by the Church, in any collective endeavor to suggest means by which the size of a family can be regulated by couples who desire to do so.

The old Malthusian formula ended up being relevant; I think it is relevant. We went through a glorious period of time when we thought that it was irrelevant. Aubrun Ward chastizes me every time I see him about it, reminding me about what he considers as axiomatic, namely, that two hands can produce more than one mouth can eat. This he feels is always true, always, always, always. He takes it as an eternal principle. I think that even if it were true it is an inconclusive observation, the conclusive one being that one must control the environment and insist on a civilized relationship with that environment. Under the circumstances, we have got to do something to compensate for the advances in hygiene and geriatrics which leave us more or less losing this particular battle.

## II. Callahan

Every couple has the moral right to plan their own family size and to employ whatever means of contraception they choose to realize those plans. In today's world, the limited family seems by and large the desirable family. Those who live in poor, underdeveloped lands probably have an obligation to keep their families very small; and that means a corresponding obligation to use an effective means of contraception. Those in affluent lands, while they may not have a special obligation socially to limit their families, will often have some very good personal and familial reasons to do so; if they do, they also should use effective contraceptives. The sexual act seems to me one which should be used primarily and most frequently for purposes of pleasure and mutual love; very rarely will it, or should it, be used for procreative purposes. If I have any worry about the use of contraceptives, it is that couples will be so psychologically geared to avoiding children that they will look upon the unexpected or "accidental" child as a disaster. I would hope that Catholics will learn how to use contraceptives and yet, all the while, retain that openness to the unexpected child which was one of the better characteristics of the old teaching. I grant that this may be extraordinarily hard to do. I think there is such a thing as a "contraceptive mentality" and I only hope Catholics will be able to use contraceptives without adopting it.

## III. DEWART

It would be difficult to deny that mankind has a generic obligation to reproduce and preserve itself: I am unaware of any serious disagreement with this view. To that extent one must agree with the traditional authoritative teaching of the Church that offspring is the essential good of marriage. But this is true only insofar as marriage is considered generically as a human institution. From this aspect of marriage it reasonably follows that individual married couples may not avoid offspring without good and sufficient reason, or without safeguarding the duties which are imposed on spouses by the other goods of marriage, which are traditionally listed as mutual fidelity and mutual sanctification. But of all the goods of marriage the latter defines the essential function of marriage and is, therefore, that which individual couples are to seek in every action of their married life—but very particularly in the essential act which is sexual intercourse. In individual marriages, therefore, the generation of offspring is not the chief end to be sought by the sexual relations of spouses. Individual couples may thus avoid offspring without avoiding sexual intercourse, if the limitation of offspring is reasonably indicated.

The conditions which make the limitation of offspring reasonable and good are not at all rare. Indeed, they have become increasingly common in modern times and must be considered normal today. The time may soon arrive, moreover, when the very good of mankind which in the past has demanded unlimited reproduction may begin to require more radical limitation than can be achieved by the unregulated decision of individual couples alone.

## IV. FRANCIS

I may differ from other contributors in this volume in that I became a Catholic in adult life. But long before I became a Catholic, even before I knew enough about the Catholic Church to know the Church opposed artificial birth control, I by my natural reason came to the conclusion that contraception was opposed to the nature of the conjugal sexual act.

Contraceptive devices seemed to me to be a denial of the integrity of the act then and they do now. Whether pills that act in a way that regulates the possibility of conception are a frustration of the integrity of the sexual act, I do not know. I can see valid arguments on both sides of the question and I would like the guidance of the magisterium of the Church on this. I have no doubt of the essential evil of the abortive pills.

I do not doubt the arguments of the demographists who say we are approaching great population problems. Perhaps I have more faith than they do in the capability of man to meet these problems.

But ultimately I would not accept the proposition that the end justifies the means. My position briefly, as a matter of personal conscience I am opposed to the use of contraceptive devices and I have been since long before I became a Catholic. I am opposed as a matter of personal conscience to pills that have an abortive effect after contraception. Concerning the use of regulative pills, where I have not formed my conscience because of lack of knowledge and an ambivalence based on what I do know, I accept the guidance of the magisterium of the Church.

Were the Pope to announce an acceptance of regulatory pills, I would have no problem in accepting this. Were the Church to approve all forms of contraception—and I think this most unlikely—I would have to accept the dictates of my conscience and hold to the position for myself that I have always held. Were the Pope to leave the matter to individual consciences, as some theologians have suggested should be done, then my conscience is already formed.

## V. MATT

With the endless progaganda that has been set in motion in recent times concerning the "population explosion" and the proposed means of curbing it, I am reminded of the apt observations made on the subject by the late Pope John XXIII in *Mater et Magistra*. The truth is, said Pope John, that we do not seem to be faced with any immediate or imminent world problem arising from the disproportion between the increase of population and the supply of food. Arguments to this effect are in fact based on such unreliable and controversial data that they can only be of very uncertain validity. Besides, the resources which God in His goodness and wisdom has implanted in Nature are well nigh inexhaustible, and He has at the same time given man the intelligence to discover ways and means of exploiting these resources for his own advantage and his own livelihood. Hence the real solution of the problem is not to be found in expedients which offend against the divinely established moral order and which attack human life at its very source, but in a renewed scientific and technical effort on man's part to deepen and extend his dominion over Nature and open new possibilities by which to house and feed and clothe people. In any case, said Pope John, "We must state most emphatically that no statement of the problem and no solution to it is acceptable which does violence to man's essential dignity" and "those who propose such solutions base them on an utterly materialistic conception of man himself and his life." The only solution to this question is one which envisages the social and economic progress both of individuals and of the whole of human society, and which respects and promotes true human values. First consideration must obviously be given to those values which concern man's dignity generally, and the immense worth of each individual human life. But the transmission of human life, through the instrumentality of man and wife in the family, "is the result of a personal and conscious act, and, as such, is subject to the all-holy, inviolable and immutable laws of God, which no man may ignore or disobey," said Pope John. Man, therefore, is not permitted "to use certain ways and means which are allowable in the propagation of plant and animal life," since "human life is sacred" and "all men must recognize that fact." "From its inception"—still quoting Pope John—"it (human life) reveals the creating hand of God" and "those who violate His laws not only offend the divine majesty and degrade themselves and humanity, they also sap the vitality of the political community of which they are members." Pope John, in this same encyclical, cites the book of Genesis by way of showing that the transmission of human life is a commandment of God Himself, who in no way gave humankind license to "destroy nature." The Pope's exclamation, "We are sick at heart, therefore, when we observe the contradiction which has beguiled so much modern thinking" on this matter, is quite understandable. "A provident God," writes Pope John, "grants sufficient means to the human race to find a dignified solution to the problems attendant upon the transmission of human life. But these problems can become difficult of solution or even insoluble, if man, led astray in mind and heart and perverted in will, turns to such means as are opposed to right reason, and seeks ends that are contrary to his social nature and the intentions of Providence."

The Pontiff's further exhortation is especially germane to the subject at issue here. He writes: "There is, alas, a spirit of hedonism abroad today which beguiles men into thinking that life is nothing more than the quest for pleasure and the satisfaction of human passions. This attitude is disastrous. Its evil effects on soul and body are undeniable. Even on the natural level temperance and simplicity of life are the dictates of sound policy. On the supernatural level, the Gospels and the whole ascetic tradition of the Church require a sense of mortification and penance which assures the rule of the spirit over the flesh, and offers efficacious means of expiating the punishment due to sin, from which no one, except Jesus Christ and His Immaculate Mother, is exempt" (*Mater et Magistra,* para. 235, May, 1961).

## VI. Sheed

That the Church has power to teach with his authority on morals was stated by Christ himself, at the Last Supper and on a mountain in Galilee.

Does the use of sex come within this power—is it a moral question, a question not only of what is wisest, best, most useful but of sin or virtue? There is no area in which men are more in need of clear guidance, none in which their judgment is so often a mask for their desire, none in which desire can so absorb and concentrate into itself all their energies. It carries with it the possibilty of the most exquisite physical pleasure, so that while it is at strength it can master a man, while making him feel that he is master. It can nourish love, it can corrode and destroy it.

Yet none of man's powers concerns the Creator so directly and continually. Among human acts the sexual is unique: no other is the channel for the continuance of the human race, no other is concerned in the production of a being that will endure everlastingly. It is sacred, since it is a co-operation with God, and a necessary co-operation—without bodily union human beings will not be conceived.

Christ gives commands upon sex—forbidding adultery, listing both adultery and fornication as things which defile a man (Mt 15: 19-20). Paul gives the seventh chapter of I Corinthians to it; calls homosexuality abominable; excommunicates a man in Corinth who has had intercourse with his father's wife, and admits him back when he repents. The Church has continued to insist upon the right use of sex whenever it is threatened.

Whether procreation is the primary purpose of *marriage* has been long discussed and Vatican II has given a most satisfyingly balanced answer. But that it is the primary purpose of *sex* calls for no discussion: sex is primarily for procreation as the heart is for the circulation of the blood: no one imagines that the intricately balanced sexual mechanism of men and women would have been there at all if they were not meant to produce children.

The Church has taught steadily that the use of sex belongs in marriage, if only because children need the stable framework of life which a permanent union of father and mother provides. Within marriage it may be used even where no more children are wanted or even possible, for it enriches that particular marriage and so strengthens the whole institution.

Upon contraception, the Church has given one single rule—that if the marriage act is used, it must be used in its integrity, not mutilated. The application of that rule to marriage today is under close consideration as I write.

# 18. DIVORCE AND REMARRIAGE

## I. BUCKLEY

I believe that divorce in the sense of a civil recognition of a separation is theologically uninteresting. What matters is whether or not one is permitted to live apart if one discovers in the evolution of a marriage an unbearable incompatibility. Such things in fact do happen. They are much more likely to happen now than they were in the past for the reason that the pressures of modern civilization are such as to concert against the kind of symbiosis which made marriages likely to succeed, if only because they tended to establish almost necessary relationships, for instance, in frontier cultures. Stability in the marriage relationship was much easier in ages when the women were never in contact with any other man, in ages when one was less aware of alternative pursuits, in ages when one didn't have the temptations that are nowadays ubiquitous, presenting themselves through television, through literature, through the movies, through travel, through whatever. Under modern circumstances it is simply unnatural to suppose that the decisions made at age 21, 22, 23 can successfully project a compatible relationship.

On the matter of remarriage, I tend to be rather orthodox. I believe that if and when the Church decides that there ought to be other grounds for permitting remarriage, other than the old grounds which went through the conduit of annulment, that the Church is wise enough to understand when those occasions occur.

I do not believe that the Church is bound to do other than to insist that the flock consider that at the moment when one individual gives his pledge to marry, he should fully intend to give it, to give it in good faith. The Church permits a nun or a priest under certain circumstances to petition for the recision of a perpetual vow of poverty; to assume that the same Church does not have the authority to permit a divorce strikes me as inconsistent. But I do believe that the emphasis of the Church is quite properly set on the permanence of the marriage vow. But it really becomes something more like the presumptive permanence of it than the binding permanence of it.

## II. CALLAHAN

The Church's presently stringent teaching on divorce and remarriage seems to me in most ways admirable. It takes seriously the binding nature of the marital commitment and forces the couple, in a generally healthy way, to work hard at keeping their relationship alive. Unfortunately, many marriages do fail, either because of mutual faults or the fault of one party; in some instances, it would be hard to say anyone was "at fault." In those cases, it seems to me divorce should be permissible, and so should remarriage. Where there are small children left adrift by a divorce, remarriage would seem to me not only moral but positively desirable. The words of Christ in Scripture on the subject, which appear to leave no loopholes for remarriage, cannot be taken as binding for all times and all marriages. They are words which have to be judged in the overall context of his ethical message; and that context would suggest that a stringent reading of his words is inadmissible. One additional point: no Catholic couple should submit their marriage problems to a Church court. They should follow their own consciences, but obliging themselves to seek counsel and help. All marriage tribunals should be dissolved; or better, be turned into marriage counseling services with no juridical authority whatever.

## III. DEWART

The traditional Catholic injunction against divorce has been understandable: the stability of marriage is greatly to be desired from every viewpoint. It is also understandable if the Church has sought to further this moral value in the direct and simple manner that has characterized social control in past ages. More attention has been given to the enforcement of a supposedly absolute prohibition against divorce (though in point of fact the Pauline privilege has always made it less than absolute), than in the development of the Catholic's consciousness of the nature of marriage and of its morality.

Divorce cannot be desirable in itself. It is, at best, a remedy for a grave evil. On the other hand, it is true that marriages sometimes break down, even to the point that it might be best for all concerned, even any children of the marriage, to discontinue any pretense that the marriage still exists. Of course, even in such cases simple separation is generally preferable to outright divorce. For in all but few cases the breakdown of a marriage involves some character defect—not necessarily of a moral nature —even in the more innocent party: a divorced person is simply not a good marriage risk. But it is necessary to admit that there are exceptions. It seems to me that for such exceptional cases adequate provision should be made.

From the viewpoint of social and ecclesiastical legislation this may be very difficult to accomplish. It is not easy to devise a legal system—least of all a canonical system—which would provide the necessary remedy without encouraging irresponsibility in the matter. Thus, any unlikely reforms which the Church might undertake in this regard would have to be coupled with a yet less likely shift in the official teaching of the Church in the direction of a morality of responsibility and creativity.

## IV. FRANCIS

"What therefore God has joined together, let no man put asunder."

I believe these words of our Lord. I do not doubt the terrible burden the strict adherence to this has placed on many persons. We live in a society that had adopted an attitude of casualness towards the marriage bond. There are many innocent parties who suffer greatly because their marriages have been dissolved and they must live alone. I have compassion for them.

There are many, I do not doubt, whose marriages have crumbled and who have committed their lives to another, in love and loyalty. I have known many such persons who have lived good lives, rearing their children in the faith from which they are cut off from the Sacraments. I have compassion for them and I pray that God will somehow reward them for their faithfulness in some things and forgive them for giving in to their human frailty.

But I would not want to see the Church change its adherence to what seems to me the clear admonition of our Lord.

## V. MATT

What is quoted above by Pope John—in the matter of contraception—applies with equal validity and force to these modern-day problems. The "spirit of hedonism," to which the Pontiff refers, is in truth the nub of the problem. As for solutions, the same Pontiff has eloquently delineated them, both on the natural as well as supernatural level, in *Mater et Magistra* and *Pacem in Terris*. It is unfortunate in the extreme that so few Catholics today bother to study these momentous pronouncements and take to heart the full import of the Papal program of social reconstruction, beginning with Pius IX on down to the present day.

## VI. SHEED

There are not many points on which Christ's teaching is clearer. In Mark (Ch. 10) and Luke (Ch. 16) he forbids divorce and remarriage as adultery. Paul (1 Cor 7) repeats the prohibition. Matthew (Chs. 5 and 19) agrees with Mark and Luke but adds a phrase "except for fornication," at whose meaning we can only guess. ("Fornication" is the sin of the unmarried and as such does not apply here. The Old Testament uses the same word for "idolatry." It may refer to a defect in the original marriage.)

Matthew and Mark show Christ as basing his exclusion of re-marriage after divorce on the word of Genesis—"They are no longer two but one. What therefore God has joined together, let no man put asunder." God does not make a couple marry, but if they do decide to marry, to take each other as husband and wife, it is God who makes them husband and wife (makes them married). That is why no earthly power can unmake them husband and wife; that is why Christ says that re-marriage of one while the other lives would be adultery.

If we had not Christ's teaching, should we see the re-marriage as wrong? Possibly not; even with his teaching plainly to be read, many Christians find that they cannot accept it. There are instances where obedience to the command causes anguish, and every natural argument seems to point to re-marriage. But Christ does not fall behind any of us in love for men. Even so stern a rule must serve love, and its breach dis-serve it.

The institution of marriage is for the health of society, for children especially. Every divorce weakens the institution. Those who stand by Christ's law at whatever cost of suffering to them-selves, bring strength to the institution and so to the community. One may feel that it is easy for a man happily married to pontif-icate. I can only register my own impression that while divorce can bring relief to individual sufferers, the flood of suffering it has let loose is beyond measure greater.

Divorce, Christ told us, had been allowed by Moses "on ac-count of the hardness of men's hearts"—they wanted something God did not want, wanted it so powerfully, that they felt unable to live by God's law. That sort of want has lost none of its power. It is not unthinkable that the Church may yet find a place within herself for those who, under a pressure they find intoler-able, re-marry after divorce. If even I have thought of a solution, I am sure that the Church can.

# 19. PRE-MARITAL SEX

## I. BUCKLEY

I see no reason at all to alter the Church's traditional stand against fornication. The observation that "everybody does it" is utterly irrelevant. It may very well be that everybody has always done it, but this seems to be nothing more than to recognize the constant allure of sin. One of the troubles of the 20th Century is that we always seek to baptize everything we do. I suppose that if enough people had killed enough Jews we would have considered that a baptized activity. The point about pre-marital sex isn't that the Church has it within its power to obliterate it but that the Church does have it in its power to continue to instruct people by saying that this is not morally permissible and that those who yield to that temptation are doing something which they ought not to do. The glory of the Church is precisely its willingness from time to time to stand up against the spirit of the age. Nothing tends to make the Church more uninteresting than to simply give it sort of a Kinseyite role as proclaiming that whatever people do we must acquiesce in as morally authorized.

## II. CALLAHAN

I find it hard to imagine many circumstances in which pre-marital sex could be considered a value; but it is quite easy to imagine circumstances under which it could be quite harmful to a couple. Hence, it seems to me the traditional Christian rule against pre-marital sex is wise and moral. But some distinctions

114

are in order. The male or female who uses sex in an exploitative way deserves the severest condemnation. The male and female, on the other hand, whose passions are simply too strong for them, or whose circumstances make physical involvement all-but-inescapable, deserve no condemnation at all. Their relationship is less than ideal in those circumstances, but is often loving and concerned. The important point in this whole area is to remove sexual "sins," other than the obviously exploitative kind, from the category of important transgressions. Rarely are they important; they are just one more way, and not one of the more significant, in which people do what it would be better if they did not do. The matter should be put in as mild terms as possible, much the way in which the Church, for instance, now deals with gluttony or inebriation. The Church has never been severe on those transgressions, and it should not be severe with pre-marital sexual transgressions. At the same time, I would add that I believe it possible for people to remain virginal without suffering any harmful consequences.

## III. DEWART

I do not believe unmarried persons should enter into sexual relations. But the meaning of this proposition must be elucidated. Consider a couple who have publicly and solemnly exchanged marriage vows according to the Catholic rite in the presence of a priest and witnesses. Such a couple is, in the absolutely strictest sense of the word, unmarried. For their resolution to marry each other has been taken as far as it can be taken, but it has not been consummated. Now, the consummation of marriage is achieved in and through sexual relations. Therefore, the statement that *only* unmarried persons should enter into sexual relations may appear startling at first consideration, but is perfectly true: it means that only unmarried persons can become married, and that they do so through the establishment of sexual relations. The point is that we should learn to think of sexual relations as antecedent, and of marriage as consequent, rather than the other way about. For instance, we should not suppose that sexual relations are permitted to married persons. It is rather the other way about: sexual relations call for the bond of marriage. Indeed, they are, to some degree or other, constitutive of the interpersonal relationship of marriage. Thus we may conclude: unmarried persons should not have sexual relations insofar as these may exclude marriage.

It may seem unnecessary to insist on the precise meaning of this statement, but the extent of the misunderstanding of Catholics on this point, even today, is difficult to exaggerate. When unmarried persons enter into sexual relations without intending marriage, what is wrong is not that they do what they are not supposed or permitted to do. What is wrong is that they distort the human meaning of their sexual congress by their (implicit or explicit) exclusion of marriage. Thus, strictly speaking, there is nothing morally wrong with pre-marital sexual relations as such. What is wrong is to have sexual relations which cannot, under the existing conditions, constitute or contribute to the couple's marriage.

This suggestion agrees in certain basic respects with the traditional position of Catholic moralists. But I also suggest that the problem has not always been adequately posed, nor its nuances sufficiently recognized: after all, sexual morality is not simpler or more clear cut than any other. It is not so much that the basic conclusions have been mistaken—though in some respects they may have been—but that the moral attitude of the Christian towards the question has been more or less seriously warped. Let us consider the matter in greater detail.

Concerning fornication, to begin with, it does not seem to me wrong because God has decreed that sexual relations must not obtain except under certain conditions reasonably and wisely disposed by him. It is wrong because it contains the intrinsic defect I have already mentioned, namely, the exclusion of marriage. And this is not a defect because God has defined marriage in a particular way, but because sexual relationships to the exclusion of marriage (at least under the historical conditions which have obtained since primitive times until our own day) positively and directly imply certain interpersonal relations which are inconsonant with being human. These are, first, the relation of the couple to any child which may result from their sexual union and, second, the relation between the two principals themselves.

We must remember that, even today, sexual relations very frequently imply a more or less remote possibility of conception. To ignore this possibility, or to exclude the intention to act accordingly if it should come to pass, cannot be described in less kind terms than utter irresponsibility for one's behaviour and total disregard of one's relations to other human beings. Of course, the day may come (and probably before very long) when the possibility of conception can be altogether removed. And even today there are not a few cases in which a condition of total and certain sterility, whether natural or artificially induced, is known to obtain. This puts a somewhat different character on the problem. If conception can be certainly ruled out, the only interpersonal relation to be considered is that between the two persons involved.

In this respect some distinctions are in order. During much of the history of our culture, the inequality in personal status between men and women has rendered fornication immoral: on the man's side because it involved a serious imposition upon another human being, and on the woman's because of her self-degradation in relation to another person. However, this is not usually the case today: fornication on a mutually friendly basis is perfectly possible nowadays, and this is a fact that Catholic moralists and the teaching of the Church should recognize. If friendly fornication remains for all that immoral (and of a degree of immorality which should be judged to be in most cases a fairly serious matter), the reason is that even the mutually benevolent basis of transitory sexual companionship and friendship is incongruous with the depth of personal involvement which sexual relations *create*. It is not by chance that despite initial mutual benevolence, sexual love affairs lightly entered into not infrequently end up with mutual recriminations and accusations of betrayal of trust.

It is necessary to deal separately with cases in which marriage is positively intended, but only in the future. If conception cannot be ruled out with absolute certainty, but the couple consciously and deliberately agree to marry (whether or not conception should follow), the irresponsibility towards the child and towards each other is not, of course, nearly as great as in any of the cases previously considered (and it may be further diminished if conception can be ruled out). Nonetheless, it may remain grave enough. To marry as a consequence of pregnancy is to marry despite the fact that, for one good reason or another (not infrequently of an economic nature) the marriage should be postponed. And sometimes the obligation to postpone the marriage may be very serious indeed. Every pregnant wedding is an indication that the marriage has been entered into as the result of an accident rather than with premeditation, and that had pregnancy not occurred the wedding would not have taken place— at least not at this time. But, if not at this time, perhaps not at all. And that is why even engaged couples who can for one reason or another exclude altogether the possibility of pregnancy should nevertheless not have sexual relations: they cannot be quite certain that they will in point of fact marry. After all, engaged couples change their minds with more than occasional frequency.

Of course, the spectrum of possible situations could be scanned beyond this point. Casuists might wonder, say, about the morality of sexual relations between a sterile couple the day before their wedding. But to pursue the discussion in this direction would take the stress away from the point I hope I have already made. I will merely repeat that sexual morality is not more clear cut or absolute than any other. And we must remember that, in the last analysis, clandestine marriages are not invalid of their very nature, but only because of an arbitrary (albeit eminently reasonable and prudent) declaration of the Church. But it is more important to emphasize that the sexual morality of engaged couples should be understood positively. For example, a couple who have sexual relations during an engagement which has been prolonged only because they cannot afford children are obviously doing wrong. For they should not postpone marriage; they should instead postpone procreation by the use of one or another reasonably effective contraceptive means.

But I would reiterate the more general point: what is wrong with those sexual relations which exclude marriage is not that in themselves they are morally abnormal sexual relations, but that (in one way or another) these sexual relations have been twisted into more or less morally abnormal interpersonal relations. The efforts of society and the Church should therefore be directed not so much to the enforcement of sexual prohibitions but to fostering the individual's understanding of his sexual responsibilities and to the society's facilitation of the sort of world in which sexual relations can more significantly contribute to mankind's individual and collective perfection. In this connection, may I add that insofar as the possibility of conception enters substantially into the morality of sexual relations among unmarried persons, the continued insistence of the Church upon the traditional teaching on contraception may itself be somewhat irresponsible.

## IV. FRANCIS

The sex act is perverted in its nature when it is not conjugal. What is one of the most beautiful and meaningful of all acts within the fulness of the commitment of two persons to each other for life becomes an act of selfishness outside of marriage.

It is a rationalization to speak of love as an excuse for premarital sex. Love requires much, it is not centered in itself, it does not seek its own gratification. What is called love as an excuse for pre-marital sexual relations is not love at all.

There is a real love in which two persons commit themselves, wholly and completely, in all ways, to each other. They then truly become one and the sexual act, which not only conveys life but deepens and broadens conjugal love, has a meaning according to its nature.

Pre-marital sex is a negation of the nature of the complete commitment integral to the act.

## V. MATT

Cf. Divorce & Remarriage, Matt.

## VI. SHEED

Pre-marital sex is fornication—the bodily union of an unmarried man and an unmarried woman. Christ lists it among the things which defile a man (Mt 15:18-19). So does St. Paul a dozen times over, e.g., I Cor 6:9: "nor shall fornicators inherit the kingdom."

Leaving Scripture out of it, "pre-marital sex" is only a parody of the real thing, indeed almost a contradiction in terms: for while the bodily act is an admirable expression of bodily union, it is not itself that union. Sexual union is not simply a joining of two bodies. It expresses the union of two persons, each wholly given to the other, not for that few minutes but for the whole of their lives together. All their shared interests, joys, sorrows, pains, pleasures, their whole selves go into it. If they share nothing but a pleasure in each other, still more if the shared pleasure is solely in the physical experience they are having together, they have not in any genuine sense had the act at all. The total giving is what makes the sexual act; and there are men who in a life of promiscuity have never had it and have remained uncleanly virginal.

# 20. RACIAL INTEGRATION

## I. BUCKLEY

I think that the bishops' statement of seven or eight years ago was correct: if segregation is practiced in a particular area because it is the feasible thing to do, if it is that which conduces to peace and the maximum development of opportunities then it is not eo ipso sinful. What is in my judgment sinful is any racist generalities that arise from segregation—racist in the sense of permitting people to believe that members of other races are inferior to themselves.

There is a burgeoning intellectual scandal going on in America regarding an imminent identification of the Negroes as having a lesser IQ than the Caucasians. I find this utterly irrelevant as a Christian and pity my non-Christian brethren who are going to be so discomfitted by it. I find it rather unreasonable because intelligence isn't all that important. Assuming it were true that the typical Negro has an IQ of 103 whereas the typical Caucasian has an IQ of 105, it is no more relevant than that the typical Irishman might have an IQ of 105, and a Jew of 108. Whoever said that intelligence was all that important? Intelligence doesn't mean that you will contribute more to your culture. I find these utterly distracting notions of interest only to a positivist society. I understand why a secularist would be disturbed, especially the ideological egalitarian. But I think that the Catholic Church ought to insist over and over and over again that the Negro is as important as the white man in the eyes of God. And if he is as important in the eyes of God, he ought certainly to be as important in the eyes of human beings.

We ought to feel required to do what we can for the Negro, but I don't think that it follows from that that the best we can do for the Negro is necessarily integration. It may in fact prove so, I don't know. But I certainly don't doubt the possibility that a team of scientists will at some point say that integration is actually contra-indicated in certain cases. Undesirable racism is an attitude that doesn't reside simply in the desire for segregation under certain circumstances, but in certain stolen bases that people take from the fact of segregation.

It is significant in the last four or five years that the Negroes in Harlem, who at one point were clamoring for integrated schools, no longer are doing so. The last poll showed that a very small percentage, something like 10 or 15%, of the students in Harlem want integrated schools. What they want is good education, and it may very well be that good education is something that they are likelier to get outside a forced integration context. But not necessarily— there are a couple of very good integrated schools in New York, very successful integrated schools. That of course is ideal.

## II. Callahan

Racial integration is clearly moral and desirable and necessary. Yet I am impressed with the "black power" advocates who claim that the Negro will never achieve his proper identity until he makes a clear and decisive break with whites and takes his destiny entirely into his own hands. I think I agree with them and think that a "black power" phase may be necessary before we can meaningfully talk of integration. If there is to be full integration someday, then the Negro must be able to dictate some of the terms, perhaps most of the terms. But he will need power to do this; and only the concept of "black power," or something like it, will likely achieve this for him. The Church's commitment to racial integration has been less than impressive. When the Church lavishes the time, money, publicity and zeal on the race issue that it now lavishes, for instance, on the parochial school system, I will be prepared to revise this judgment.

## III. DEWART

In what pertains to the restricted, domestic import of this question, little remains to be said at the level of theory and of principle. What is needed is above all action.

The larger and, indeed, in the long run even more pressing problem, however, has received less attention. I refer to the problem of the integration of mankind on a planetary basis. Relatively few Catholics yet realize that nationalism is a form of racism, and that it is no less immoral and unchristian than the domestic variety because its basis is political rather than biological, or because it discriminates on an international rather than a more restricted scale. The catholicity of the Christian faith creates, under contemporary historical conditions, a world-political vocation to which the Church is not, apparently, as yet fully awake.

## IV. FRANCIS

Our goal must be a society in which the pigmentation of the skin makes no more difference than the color of the eyes or of the hair.

We have failed so miserably in the past, our white prejudices have been so prevalent, that black men have learned the lessons of our racism and have adopted a racism of their own.

To retrieve a situation that could bring about a racially divided nation, the white power structure must move with massive means to eliminate the social injustices and inequities born of white racism.

Whatever discriminates against a man because of the color of his skin must be eliminated—in housing, in education, in job opportunities. Because we have waited so long we must undertake a drastic program to rectify the errors of the past as quickly as possible.

At the same time, the society of the whole must prevent riots, destruction, guerilla warfare. If the hopelessness that leads to such violence is of our own making and can be understood, it cannot be condoned. If out of a sense of guilt—which we rightfully feel—we excuse and condone the violence then we will finally wind up with a chaos that will destroy the very framework of law and order that must support the integrated society we must bring about.

## V. Matt

This is a question I leave to the experts—among whom I do *not* include agitators and fomentors of discord such as Rap Brown, or Stokely Carmichael. The Christian answer to revolution, to tyranny, to injustice and oppression in any form, was perhaps best demonstrated by such genuine Christian social reformers as St. Charles Borromeo. The latter was singled out by St. Pope Pius X as having removed himself "as far as possible from those false reformers who work their obstinate disobedience under the appearance of zeal," or who would "renew human society after their own fashion, by overturning everything, by agitation, by vain noise, forgetting the Divine caution that 'the Lord is not found in commotion.'" Racial peace and harmony will not be restored by such as these!

## VI. McLuhan

The concept of racial integration is a rear-view mirror idea of a highly literate society. Colored people don't desire integration but autonomy. I visited an institute for the blind recently. There the concept of teaching and instruction for the blind is exactly the same as that which used to be administered to the left-handed. All left-handed people used to be taught right-handedness as soon as they went to school. The blind are mainly instructed in how to behave as if they could see. Instead of taking advantage of the fact that the blind have other senses that are very much sharper than those of the sighted, and instead of instructing them with special stress on the benefits which they enjoy from their blindness, all energy is devoted to dealing with them as cripples who should be able to simulate sightedness and a full possession of their senses.

One little girl in the group that we talked with about their experience was a colored girl, and she said, "Wouldn't it be wonderful if everyone was blind so there would be no race problem?" The concept of integration is like that—it's a literate concept of imposing a uniform pattern of behavior and outlook and sensibility on everybody, so that the Negro who enjoys many cultural and sensory advantages which the literate community lack is dealt with as a defective person who should be made to simulate all of the characteristics of white society. Instead of being allowed to express and develop his unique sensory powers and characteristics, he is expected to conform to visual culture. The non-white races know this now and realize that "integration" is a false and illusory kind of goal since it is one that appeals to the ideal of visual homogeneity that is natural to highly literate Western man.

## VII. SHEED

Racial integration is an odd phrase. It would seem to mean that coloured people should be admitted to that integrated society which the whites now have. But of course they haven't. Our society is a mass of segregations—between haves and have-nots, based upon the having or the lacking of wealth, education, acceptable social habits. In practice what Racial Integration means is that skin colour should no longer be a ground of exclusion or rejection—that the colour of his skin should make no more difference to a man's social or political acceptance and advancement than the colour of his eyes.

For Christians the decisive consideration is what man is—he is a union of matter and spirit, by his spirit immortal, made in God's image, and Christ died for him. No matter what a mess may have been made of a given man by maltreatment from others or his own sins, these are the plain facts about every man. In their light, the statement that all men are equal makes total sense; the natural qualities by which men differ are a trifle compared with these vast matters common to all. The Christian view of man is one view in which every man is an object of respect simply for being a man.

This does not mean that all men are equally fitted for every function. But in so far as the unfitness of any group is the result of past or present maltreatment, our every instinct should be to labor for its renewal. And meanwhile any given man should be valued for what he in fact is rather than for what we suppose his group lacks.

# 21. ANTI-SEMITISM

## I. Buckley

I wrote a couple of years back about the anti-anti-Semitic promulgation of Vatican II. I understand why it was made historically. The Church obviously wanted to absolve itself from any implicit participation in the genocide of the forty's. At the same time it struck me as overly abject and rather self conscious. I do not understand that anti-Semitism is built into Christian doctrine except in the sense that there is inbuilt in Christian doctrine an anti-Buddhist position, anti-Druidic position, anti-any position that isn't Christian. It is true that some people who have sought to pursue anti-Semitism seem to feel that they are emboldened to do so by certain tendencies, certain remarks in the New Testament and by certain interpretations of them by Church Fathers (incidentally and not widely known is Martin Luther's anti-Semitic virulence) but I don't think they were ever incorporated into Church dogma. I think that anti-Semitism is obviously wrong but I regret Christianity going so far, so far as it sometimes seems to be going, as to sacrifice what I assume is the proper pride of a religion that believes in itself as the true religion, by a sort of relativist endiamence towards other religions which we are bound by dogma to consider as false.

## II. Callahan

I have not been impressed with the recent exegetical attempts to show that anti-semitism cannot be traced back to Scripture. On

127

the contrary, anti-semitism seems to me to have been built into Christianity from the very beginning; and it will continue to be part of Christianity so long as we talk of an "Old" and a "New" Testament. Now, however, I think there is a genuine desire to overcome anti-semitism. This desire would be facilitated, not by attempts to show that somehow anti-semitism is an accidental wart on the body of the Church (some accidents occur too frequently to be laid to sheer chance), but to admit that Christianity may now be wiser than it was in the beginning; in other words, to repudiate rather than explain away those passages in Scripture which have provided an apparent warrant for anti-semitism.

## III. DEWART

Insofar as anti-semitism is a form of racism, the comments made above apply here without qualification. However, the Jews are not only an ethnic group: they are also a religious group, a spiritual nation and, indeed, the prototype of the Christian Church. Now, the catholicity of the Christian faith calls not only for a commitment to the racial, social and political integration of mankind: it also creates a vocation to contribute to the religious development of mankind as a whole. Thus, in a world increasingly characterized by the self-organization of man on a planetary scale, the catholicity of the Christian faith also implies a vocation to an ecumenical (as contrasted with a merely provincial) ecumenism. A truly ecumenical ecumenism seeks the religious integration of mankind.

This is, of course, hardly a novel suggestion. But in the past the missionary vocation of the Christian faith has been very narrowly understood as proselytism. And the evangelical mission has been conceived as implying not only that Christianity had a unique and distinctive claim to truth (and hence a unique and distinctive contribution to offer to man) but also an exclusive one (and hence an exclusive right to man's religious allegiance). In what may well turn out to be its most consequential and revolutionary doctrines, Vatican II disposed of this view—hopefully once for all.

The Catholic Church must in the first place seek integration (not necessarily uniformity or juridical unity) within itself, that is, it must seek to integrate its Roman Catholic, Protestant and Eastern components. In due course, the three semitic-scriptural religions, Judaism, Christianity and Islam, must likewise seek integration in some form which cannot as yet be usefully defined. Beyond that remains the goal of integration (in some valid sense of this term) with the higher religions of the Far East.

These suggestions should not be divorced from those made in the previous section on racial integration. The *Catholic* (and I do not mean only the Roman) Church cannot very well be expected to assume a catholic-religious role except to the same degree that it becomes involved in a catholic-political and a catholic-social role.

## IV. FRANCIS

A Catholic who would be anti-semitic is totally irrational. To curse Jews and ask the prayers of the Jewish mother of Our Lord is schizophrenic. Yet there are Catholic anti-semites—any one who writes against anti-semitism in the Catholic press soon learns this from the hate letters he receives.

The declaration of Vatican II should never have been necessary —if we do not understand that our sins crucified Him we haven't understood the meaning of His redemptive death. But it was good that the Council fathers spoke. Whatever must be done to turn Catholics from the sin of anti-semitism should be done.

## V. MATT

As Christians and Catholics, we are, as Pius XI reminded us long ago, "spiritually Semites." Consequently, no man who calls himself Christian can be anti-Semitic—nor, for that matter, can Christians hate or despise any man because of race or nationality or creed. In this question as in all others wherein we may disagree, and are oftentimes forced to disagree with the attitudes and philosophies of men, we strive to follow always the ancient dictum of St. Augustine: "Hate the sin, love the sinner."

It is a matter for us Catholics to be especially proud that the

Second Vatican Council, in its Declaration on the Relation of the Church to Non-Christian Religions, spoke out so clearly and directly on the question of anti-semitism as well as all forms of discrimination based on race, color, class or creed. In that statement the Church emphasized her condemnation of "all persecutions of any men; she remembers her common heritage with the Jews and, acting not from any political motives, but rather from a spiritual and evangelical love, deplores all hatred, persecutions and other manifestations of antisemitism, whatever the period and whoever was responsible." The same declaration (para. 5) tells us that "we cannot call on God, the Father of all men, if there are any men whom we refuse to treat as brothers." It stresses the fact that "there are no grounds for any theory or practice which leads to discrimination between men or races in matters pertaining to the dignity of man, and the rights which stem from it."

I say we Catholics may be proud of the above and we would be well advised to let our Jewish compatriots know of the initiative our Church has taken here and ask them, in turn, to reciprocate in kind. For if it be true, as the Vicomte Leon De Poncins points out in his book *Judaism and the Vatican* (London, 1967), that one of the principal personalities who brought the Jewish question to the attention of the Council—Jules Isaac—holds the four Evangelists to be rank liars, our Church Fathers perverters and torturers who spread hatred of the Jews and were the precursors of Hitler and Streicher and were in fact responsible for Auschwitz and Buchenwald—then it would seem that we Catholics are being poorly paid for our tolerance and leading Jews of today are taking advantage of our gullibility. Tolerance is a two-way street.

## VI. McLUHAN

The Jews are a tribal people. As the world retribalizes through electric means of involvement, the intense intolerance that each tribal society feels for all other tribes has begun to manifest itself even in those civilized or detribalized areas that had been supposed to be free from tribal passions. The tribe lives in the dream of the unity and purity of all its members. Such is the ideal of the Church at a spiritual level. Tribal cultures bitterly resent intrusions into their language or culture or rituals. That is why they are static rather than progressive. Paradoxically, the natural terminus of rapid change is total stasis when the slightest variation from ritual norms is shunned. The modern world is approaching this condition very rapidly. The tribalism that Hitler and Mussolini reawakened was achieved by radio. The tribalism involved and inherent in TV is far greater, as appears in our youngsters today. If literate man is being retribalized by his electric technology, the tribal parts of the world are being confirmed and strengthened in their tribalism. The Negro is "turned on" by electricity. He experiences Black Power or tribal unity and depth of communion. Literate Western man is "turned off" by electricity, experiencing disunity and confusion of all his past ideals.

Another of the many paradoxes relating to tribalism is its great difference from the visual conformity insisted upon by literate or visual men. Homogeneity does not require the centralism of structure necessary to civilize societies. Since tribalism is an inner rather than an outer state, it can be felt intensely without physical proximity. Visually cultured or civilized people need not only central organization but physical proximity in order to achieve their social values. This is a fact that puzzles parents today with regard to their retribalizing children. They accuse the tribal young of being mere conformists when the inner states which the young are seeking have very little to do with their visual appearance.

Since semitism is tribal, the anti-semitism of the detribalized man is utterly confused. Semitism is based not so much on culture as on religion, and the civilized man dedicated to de-tribalizing has been utterly baffled by Jewish tribalism as much as by Christian tribalism. Thus, the anti-semitism of the Roman bureaucrat was a very different thing from the anti-semitism of the electronically retribalized Hitler. In such conflicting components it is easy to see the possibilities of endless confusion. Paradoxically, again, it is the confusion and uncertainty of images that engenders the impulse to violence. When identity becomes unsure, violence offers itself as a means of reassurance. Seen as the quest for identity, violence becomes at least understandable, whether in its anti-semitism or anti-Negro or anti-any other factor in the confusion of identity. Only those supremely sure of their identity can totally dispense with violence as a means to the ascertaining of identity. The Christian alone is potentially in such a position.

## VII. SHEED

My concern is not with anti-Semitism as a world-wide phenomenon, but solely with the hatred of Jews as slayers of Christ. What was their part in Christ's death? On the face of it, one would say that it would be impossible to imagine any crime committed nineteen hundred years ago for which the descendants of the criminals still merited massacre. Even if every member of the race had been involved in the original crime, seventy generations seems a long while for guilt to persist. But what reason is there to think that the whole of the Jewish nation was involved in the handing over of Christ to the Roman official who had him crucified by Roman soldiers?

In Christ's time there were more Jews living outside Palestine than inside. So the majority of Jews living at the time knew nothing of the crime. What of the Jews in Palestine? The Sanhedrin which finally handed him over to Pilate had seventy members: we know that some of these, like Nicodemus and Joseph of Arimathea, were on His side. We must not be misled by thinking of the Sanhedrin as the governing body and therefore entitled to speak for the Jewish people; they were Sadducee in majority, collaborators with the pagan Roman conquerer, and the high priests were Roman appointees.

What did the great mass of the people in Jerusalem at the time of his death think about Christ? We have one solid piece of evidence: His enemies did not dare to have Him arrested in the daytime for fear of the populace. The morning of His death found a crowd gathered round Pilate's judgment seat, clamoring for His crucifixion. It is quite fantastic what has been built upon that crowd. We do not know who they were or what their number: they give a certain air of having been brought there to shout against Christ. But for the rest we know nothing of them. Yet their cry "His blood be on our heads and on our children's heads" has been treated by so many Christians through the ages as a solemn pronouncement of the Jewish race, justifying the slaughter of any Jew anywhere.

We do know something about the numbers of those Jews of the time who accepted Our Lord—there were a hundred and twenty in the Upper Room when the Holy Ghost came upon them; St. Paul tells us that after His resurrection, Christ appeared to five hundred of them at one time. Have we any solid ground for believing that His enemies among the Jews numbered more? And how can any Christian forget the gifts beyond measure Israel has given us?

# 22. ECUMENICAL MOVEMENT

## I. BUCKLEY

The ecumenical movement is something with which I confess sort of a visceral impatience. It does seem to me that in fact it has resulted in the dilution of the strength of Christianity. I am all in favor, and who isn't, of perpetual concordats with people who disagree with us, or who adopt other faiths, or whatever. I had no difficulty, and presumably you had no difficulty and other people had no difficulty, in getting along with Protestants and Jews before Vatican II. The terribly disappointing thing about the ecumenical movement is that from the moment that it started not only did the Catholic Church lose its strength but also the Protestant Churches lost strength. As in the case of the liturgical reforms those promises which were held out to us of great Christian advances as result of ecumenical zeal in fact did not materialize.

I think the reason they did not materialize is because somewhere along the line most people begin to think of Christianity as a social movement. If it is a social movement it is a bore. It either is a supernatural movement, or people would go around, as indeed a lot of them have, and select a "religion" that is more nearly tailor made. They would move around eclectically and take a little bit of Thoreau, a little bit of Plato, a little bit of Proust, and a little bit of St. Theresa and mix it all up and say "This is my warm puppy." I just think that from almost any point of view the ecumenical movement has failed. I suppose one can identify here and there an inchoate Paul Blanshard who says "I am satisfied of the good offices of the Catholic Church now that the local priest has presided over a folk Mass and persuaded me that there isn't anything one really needs to take seriously in the Catholic Church." But this isn't in my judgment what Catholicism is about. The Catholicism that I take seriously takes itself seriously.

## II. CALLAHAN

I have now ceased to have much interest in the "ecumenical movement" as such mainly because in my work, my research and in my group of close friends and colleagues, it is taken totally for granted. I assume this will be the case with everyone else before long. The reunion of the churches would, I suppose, be desirable, but I am continually impressed with the creative possibilities of the present pluralism within Christianity. If we could continue that pluralism in the midst of reunion, I would have no objection. If there is "one true Church," it is probably the community of all Christians; how they organize themselves seems to me of secondary importance.

## III. DEWART

In the preceding section I have already commented on ecumenism properly so-called—that is, what Raymond Panikkar has called ecumenical ecumenism. But ecumenism in the provincial, intra-Christian sense is more pressing, precisely because it is a more restricted, more immediate and much more feasible form of Christian Catholicism. In this respect two considerations seems to me worthy of attention.

First, ecumenical integration need not, indeed should not, mean amalgamation. And it may not, indeed cannot, mean re-union, that is, a return to the state of original indifferentiation. The plurality of forms of genuine Christian belief must be in some way retained *within* the Catholic (i.e. Christian) Church as well as in the larger context of world-ecumenism. For this reason full Christian intercommunion seems to me a particularly important goal for which to strive. Ecumenical integration within Christianity may turn out to be like a sort of spiritual world-citizenship within a closely federated system of member churches.

Second, an ecumenical Church must be built from the ground

up. Its construction begins not at the top, but at the level of everyday Christian life, from which it proceeds to theological, juridical and other discussion. For the foundation of the *Catholic* Church is the faith by which a man hopes and loves—and faith is most radically embodied not in doctrine, speculative or otherwise, or in juridical structures, but in the believer's self-disposition towards the future in which he hopes, and towards the present to which he gives himself.

## IV. Francis

Our Lord has said we will be one. I believe this.

There are those who say it is necessary for Christians to unite because of the rising danger of Communism and Godlessness. I reject this because it is negative. We are not called on to huddle together in the face of some danger. We are called upon to seek one another in truth and in love.

Christians have been divided by sin—by arrogance, pride. We are called upon to love one another and it is our love for God and each other that should motivate our efforts to come closer to one another.

In an important sense, the ecumenical movement must embrace all men. We are called upon to love all men, not only those who are closest to us. In a practical way, we are already close to those with whom we share Christian baptism and love of Our Lord Jesus Christ so it follows that our first searchings begin with those with whom we already share some degree of unity.

It is good that we emphasize our likenesses, the things we share in common, but we must not hide from our differences. We are separated by our differences and we must seek to resolve them.

It is good that theologians should discuss those differences but finally, if it is to be successful, the ecumenical movement must involve all men. If not all men can discuss theological differences, all men can offer love and respect for those who are separated from them.

It seems to me the ecumenical movement of Catholics has all too often shut out that great body of Protestant Christians who are fundamentalists or new evangelicals. We hold so much in common with them that it is a tragedy that we do not reach out to them more. It is true that among these Christians there are those who consider the Catholic Church a great evil—well, if they will not reach out to us this does not excuse us from not reaching out to them.

Nothing in the ecumenical movement should imply indifferentism. One of the weaknesses of the current movement is that so many involved are theological liberals who, believing little, find it easy to make an approach since nothing in their approach involves contradiction of their own commitments.

The movement towards Christian unity should demand of no one compromise with what he holds to be true. But men committed to contradictory theological opinions can open themselves to one another in love and friendship and open themselves to the Holy Spirit that the Holy Spirit, working in an atmosphere of love and respect, might bring men to the Christian unity they could not gain for themselves alone.

## V. MATT

The idea of uniting our energies and consolidating our forces in the face of a common peril is, of course, perfectly reasonable and sound. Jews, Protestants and Catholics alike, and all men of good will, are realizing that the world is serving their souls with an awful summons—the summons to heroic efforts at spiritualization. An alliance, however, among Jews, Protestants and Catholics is not necessary—as Bishop Fulton J. Sheen once pointed out (*Communism and the Conscience of the West*), to fight against an *external* enemy—for our "wrestling is not against flesh and blood; but against principalities and powers, against the rulers of the world of this darkness, against the spirits of wickedness in the high places." What Bishop Sheen wrote about this matter (in 1948) is still pertinent and valid today: "We desire unity of religion but not when purchased at the cost of the unity of the truth. But we plead for a unity of religious people, wherein each marches separately according to the light of his conscience, but strikes together for the moral betterment of the world; a unity through prayer, not hate. . . . We may not be able to meet in the same pew —would to God we could—but we can meet on our *knees*. (However) no sordid compromise, nor carrying waters on both shoulders will see us through."

Pope Paul, in a variation of the same theme, tells us (*Ecclesiam Suam*): "The desire to come together as brothers must not lead to a watering-down or subtracting from the truth. Our dialogue (with our separated brethren) must not weaken our attachment to our Faith. In our apostolate we cannot make vague compromises about the principles of faith and action on which our profession of Christianity is based. An immoderate desire to make peace and sink differences at all costs is, fundamentally, a kind of skepticism about the power and content of the Word of God which we desire to preach. Only the man who is completely faithful to the teaching of Christ can be an apostle. And only he who lives his Christian life to the full can remain uncontaminated by the errors with which he comes in contact."

In brief, we must *not*, in our efforts to restore health to a dangerously sick society, risk catching the disease. Our job is to convert the world, not to be converted to it!

## VI. McLuhan

Ecumenism is not a concept but a percept. As an idea, of course, it has everything to recommend it but nothing to win it acceptance. Ecumenism is an inevitable accompaniment of any instantaneous communication system. When you live in daily association with the members of every other religion on earth, the mosaic that forms in your own consciousness is not unlike that of the front page of a newspaper. There are no connections but it is all under one dateline. The disparate items derive their unity from the instantaneous means of coexistence which we have created electrically. One of the mysteries of mosaic is that "being in touch" does not create connections but intervals. Tactility is not continual. "To the blind all things are sudden." It is only to the sense of sight that there is a continual. To all the other senses experience is discontinuous. Again, paradoxically, it is the interval that creates the means of involvement. We feel the need to complete or close each interval, each gap in experience. It is this closure that creates our involvement. Where only the visual sense is concerned and all things are connected, there is detachment rather than involvement. It is thus the mystery of ecumenism that by creating much more involvement it also places more stress on diversity and uniqueness and autonomy.

In an instantaneous world there is no past, because all the pasts are present, and there is no time since everything is always now. Instantaneous information movement as a perceptual fact of our everyday existence is an overwhelming reality. Thus, ecumenism is a pattern which now extends to every form of political and social life on this planet. It is not something that characterizes the Church as such.

## VII. SHEED

For four centuries Catholics and Protestants based their relations not on the 75% on which they were agreed, but on the 25% of difference. Pope John exposed the abysmal folly of this when he said of the other Christian bodies, "They bear the name of Christ on their forehead." This is the primary fact about all the Churches: because of it they must accept each other not as rivals but as men who love Christ and are loved by him.

But the differences remain—genuine differences as to what Christ wanted men to believe and to do. And these are no matter for compromise or diplomacy. The only reason for holding them at all is the conviction that they are Christ's will for men. While we see them so, we must hold to them. Seeing the Catholic faith so, I would want a Baptist to have it too: if the Baptist is the man I think he is, he would feel the same desire to share with me the beliefs he prizes as Christ's.

The union of hearts has begun, and apart from the hardness of men's hearts, there is nothing to keep it from growing to the limit. The union of minds *must* be slower, but a genuine union of hearts will help it, and indeed a respect for what the other group holds will help the union of hearts. Truth must not be ecumenism's first victim.

And here I must admit to a foreboding. I have frequented Inter-Faith meetings and it is rare to find Christ discussed, or even, after the opening prayer, much mentioned. All reverence him but there is the widest difference among them as to who and what he is—the Second Person of the Trinity made man, a man sent by God, a witness to God in human nature, a first century Jew of unequalled spiritual genius, a man around whom splendid stories have clustered (with the miracles all the truer for not having happened). There seems to be a feeling that discussion of Christ would cause division: but the division is already there, polite ignoring will not heal it. While it remains, union of hearts and union of minds must suffer. "What think ye of Christ?" is still the first question.

# 23. LITURGICAL CHANGES IN THE YEARS IMMEDIATELY AHEAD

## I. BUCKLEY

I would welcome any liturgical changes in the years ahead. I can't imagine things getting any worse. As a matter of fact, a priest who is close to the liturgical neo-theorists tells me that they are actually considering having us clasp hands with the people to our right and to our left in the pews. I hope that will be aborted before St. John's of Minnesota or whoever it is that has imposed this profanation on us has its way.

Once again just viewed empirically it seems to me that the changes in the liturgy are ineffective, taking only the example of my own Church. We now, after three and a half years, have arrived, the thousand of us who fill that Church, the largest in Connecticut, at a point where nobody sings the hymns. We started with a hundred and went down at a rate of about 25% per year and then finally we reached the apogee a few weeks ago when nobody sang at all. So we go through this "We will now sing the entrance hymn" and the organ plays. But nobody sings.

I have been persuaded, even after a rather rancorous outburst against the vernacular, that there is a case to be made for the vernacular. But the vernacular must be made musical. Which means that you have to destroy, preferably by fire, all existing translations. Destroy those we have been given in church and go back to translations made by people who know English. People like Monsignor Knox.

The notion that the Mass is a bilateral engagement is one which

I think is interesting psychologically but which I also find empirically unrelated to the American culture. I have seen situations in which the flock in fact contributes to the saying of the Mass. I saw it just once, namely in Portsmouth Priory School where you can get a programmed response from the students because they are practiced in this and they do what they are told. But a long experience in a passive relationship between the congregation and the priest is an identifying part of our experience and in my judgment therefore reforms ought to take into account the fact of that relationship and ought not to ask the congregation to do what it is manifestly unwilling to do. I deeply lament some of the sacrifices that have been made on the altar of that histrionic ideal. For instance, what seems to have been an almost over-night dropping of the missal. It takes years and years to train people to read the missal and now they don't even read it. They just plain flat don't read it. They just sit around and don't sing hymns and bop up and down as if they were in a night club. They are constantly distracted by meaningless and utterly uncommunicative objurgations by the lector, of which I was one for three years in an attempt to play by the rules. I think that the whole thing is an absolute mess. I do think that it is true that a lot of new liturgists believe that it is a mess. They believe that it's got to change. However they tend to want to change by going further and further away from that which was satisfactory to St. Thomas More and Cardinal Newman. They want to experiment some more. Maybe we should be grateful that they recognize that the existing system is no good, but sorry that pride seems to foreclose their exhausting the possibilities of ambling back toward some of that which was good in the past.

## II. CALLAHAN

One of the great, but generally unrecognized, misfortunes of the past few decades has been the liturgical movement. The misfortune does not lie in the movement itself or its aims (a relevant, understandable, flexible liturgy), but in the amount of energy it has displaced from more important projects, and in its misplacement of fundamental Christian values. The liturgy should never have been considered the source and the center of the Christian life. It is important, indeed vital, but it shares its importance with many other aspects of Christian life. By staking so much on liturgical reform, and by making it the key to all other reforms, the liturgical movement has provided people with a means of evading the full responsibilities of their Christian life in the world. In theory, this is not supposed to happen; the liturgy is supposed to give people the strength and power to be more effective and authentic in the world. But this theory breaks down in practice because the psychological impact of an emphasis on liturgy is that of providing people with an alternative to service in the world. Thus the Christ we can encounter in our neighbor has been subordinated to the Christ we encounter in the Eucharist; but the former is just as important as the latter. I am convinced that full Christian service in the world will not psychologically become possible until the liturgy is radically devaluated. Such a devaluation should not be taken to mean a slighting of liturgy or an end to liturgical reform. It only means placing it in the broader context of the whole Christian life; it is this broader context which should determine our concern with liturgy. The emphasis of the liturgical movement has been to judge the whole Christian life in liturgical terms, thus reversing the priority which should be decisive. A practical corollary of this reversal of priorities would mean: a) "churches" would not be built for purposes of worship, but rather as centers of human service and community; there would be worship in the churches, but this would be casual and celebrative and reconciliating—it would not be the center of the church's life, but only a symbol of it. b) Matters of liturgical reform and liturgical law would be relatively insignificant items, mainly left to the wishes and needs of local congregations. c) Extraordinary care would be taken not to allow the liturgy to become overritualized. Ritual can have an important place in human life; but it can also serve as an escape from life. To ensure that the latter does not happen, there should be few set times for liturgical worship, no set places, and relatively few set rubrics. The psychological point of this kind of flexibility would be to indicate to the people that their Christian life must never be allowed to center in the liturgy; instead, liturgy should be an occasion of joy, thoroughly mixed with the rest of their life.

## III. DEWART

The most important liturgical change of the millenium has already occurred. For the first time in 1,000 years the language of the Roman liturgy is the language of the everyday life of its participants. And the vernacular languages are not only living and intelligible: they also (a) reflect contemporary experience, (b) undergo rapid change, and (c) take many forms, geographically and culturally conditioned. Thus, every other liturgical change for a very long time to come is bound to be anticlimactic —not in the sense that changes will be unimportant or even unspectacular, but in the sense that they will be but a consequence of the crucial change that has already taken place.

Having but recently adopted the vernacular we are, of course, in a period of experimentation and rapid transition. Stable liturgical forms will not be forthcoming for a long time—perhaps they never will. But if and when they do come, their stability will not consist in either immutability or uniformity, but in the Church's mastery over the process of conscious self-development.

Among the principal lines of development which will have to be seriously studied in the near future is the possible repatriation of all liturgical celebrations to their natural location in everyday life. The most obvious of these is the private home. But every human habitat—the park, the lecture hall, the public auditorium, the theatre, the street, and so on—will have its peculiar advantages under given concrete conditions. This is already an established trend. Its logical extrapolation would lead, with apt symbolism, to a total moratorium on the construction of new churches and other liturgically sacred buildings.

## IV. FRANCIS

Whatever brings man into closer communication with God has my enthusiastic support. Twenty-two years ago I favored the vernacular because it seemed obvious to me that a great many people were simply going through the motions, that they were repeating formulas but not coming into a real encounter with God.

Now I'm not one of those who thinks change in itself is either good or bad, it can be either. There is a certain go-go attitude towards liturgical change that doesn't seem to me altogether healthy. Some of it approaches fadism.

The first guitar Mass in which I participated was wonderful. It was in a context that was natural. The music was folk music and the people who participated in that folk Mass were mountain people to whom the instrument and the melodies were natural.

The next guitar Mass in which I paricipated was horrible. It involved people who were playing a game. There was nothing natural about it. It embarrassed many of the people who were participating and those it didn't embarrass should have been embarrassed.

Since then I've attended several times a youth Mass where guitars are used. They were subdued, the music was natural and fit the context. I was almost unaware that it was a guitar Mass at all.

The aim of the liturgy should be joyful worship, derived naturally from the people's desire to praise the Lord. Some of the liturgical changes are much too intense, too joyless, proceeding not organically but by imposition.

I'll be glad to have any liturgical changes that proceed naturally and joyfully from our need to come to a fuller encounter with God. I suppose that means there must be some experimentation but I think there must be some control over experimentation. I think we finally need to move as the whole People of God and I'd not like to see the community of the People of God fragmented by movements in a thousand different directions.

I have no qualms about movements that involve separate groups of people. But again I think some caution is needed. For example, I'm not altogether happy about special youth Masses. Of all the classifications of man, youth is the most transitory. We need to learn to worship together, not in little pigeon-holes of transitory classifications.

Perhaps this isn't intended to be the place to discuss it but the experimental parishes don't seem to me quite in harmony with my understanding of the People of God. I don't want just to worship in community with people just like me. My understanding of community is broader than this; it includes all, the old and the young, the rich and the poor, the educated and the poor, the black skin and the pink skin.

## V. MATT

Our liturgists, it seems to me, have become so obsessed with external changes that they thereby indict themselves of interior emptiness, if not complete bankruptcy of the spirit. What they forget, if they ever understood at all, is that the Mass is after all—as our Lord Himself said—a Mystery (*Mysterium Fidei*), and there is no language, no external rite or rubric, that can make the Mass "understandable" or "meaningful" unless the Holy Spirit wills it.

If there is one more change that I should like to see, therefore, it would be a change on the part of priests and people away from lectors and commentators and all finite creatures and back to the focal point of our worship, which is or should be God!

## VI. McLUHAN

The new religious stress on liturgy or public participation is paralleled by many developments in the arts. The need for involvement, after ages of spectatorship and non-involvement, creates this desire for participation in an active way which we associate with the liturgical revival. The concept of corporate action and the satisfactions to be derived from corporate worship are very much a part of the new electric time with its inevitable pattern of co-existence and closer involvement. The consumer age which preceded the electric age was not one of participation. Rather, it was one of detachment, objectivity and separateness resulting from the merely visual culture of literate stress and of mechanical production and consumption. In an age which stresses the service environment of an information type, the whole of political and social life takes on a ritualistic character which makes for a kind of public liturgy in all things. So I would say again that as with ecumenism, the liturgical revival is following a secular cultural pattern, i.e. it is totally pervasive in this time. The key term in this electric time is involvement, the sense of total responsibility not only for one's own acts but for the acts of many others, and this sharpens the awareness of the advantages of liturgical prayer and liturgical participation in all forms of worship and of social action.

## VII. SHEED

In heaven Christ continues His offering of himself, once slain on Calvary, now forever living, to his heavenly Father—for the application to men of the Redemption he won for the race (Hebr. 7: 24-5).

The Mass is the breaking through to our altars of this intercession—the priest, in the name and in the power of Christ, offers the same Christ—once slain, now forever living—to the same Heavenly Father for the same purpose. We of the laity are lifted into the splendour of this action—"my sacrifice and yours," says the priest. Compared with what Christ and the priest and we are joined in doing, details of vestments or street clothes, church or somebody's kitchen table, ancient language on vernacular are secondary—not unimportant, but not primary. They will be good or less good, according as they express the mind and heart of the worshippers. The danger is, of course, that the liturgical experts may take over: and they are more likely than not to be out of touch with the mind and heart of the rest of us. If we all come to a living awareness of what is being done at the altar and of our part in it, there will be a change in the congregation which will do more than any number of changes in the rituals.

# 24. WHAT WILL THE ROMAN CATHOLIC CHURCH BE LIKE IN THE YEARS AHEAD?

## I. BUCKLEY

I think that what is likely is that a great number of people who have believed that they will find satisfaction in a Church which is dogmatically jejune will find otherwise. At that point a lot of energies which heretofore have gone into works of "liberalizing the Church" will go rather into a husbanding of its crystallized dogmatic and magisterial resources. How large the Church will be at that point I don't know. I am utterly and totally and sublimely confident a) that it will endure, and b) that it will continue to cast even a decisive vote in the moral councils of the civilized community. I don't know what the Holy Ghost has in store for us, whether through this Pope or his successor, but I do really believe that it will be exhilarating and that the diaspora of the Catholic Church will assert itself and re-invest the Church with something of a meaning which seems temporarily to be lost.

It may be that we are over-mellodramatizing what has happened during this period. Certainly the objective indices are discouraging: the loss of vocations, the latitudinarianism, the sort of relaxed relationship towards the Church. But who knows, maybe fifty years from now the salient factor of the mid-Twentieth Century will not be the apparent collapse of the Church during the 60's but its rejuvenation in the 70's and 80's.

148

## II. CALLAHAN

Since doctrine and discipline often seem to follow practice, I suspect that the Church will be far more flexible and open in the years ahead. This seems almost inevitable since so many Catholics (particularly the younger ones) are themselves open and flexible. As they mature, the Church is likely to take on their coloration. Practically speaking, this means that the Church's teaching authority will shape itself to those it attempts to teach. The Church is a very practical institution; it will do what it has to do to survive, and that means allowing the dissent, heterodoxy and untrammeled speculation which is increasingly being demanded and practiced in the Church. I do not foresee any major formal schisms, except perhaps from the right. As a tool of reform, the formal schism is historically discredited; it may provide psychological release, as well as a sense of Christian integrity of conscience; but, as a tool of reform, its use seems historically very limited. There will, though, be many informal schisms— many underground churches—but these churches are likely to continue thinking it important to remain in creative tension with the institutional church; and the institutional Church is likely to reciprocate. Assuming that the Church continues to reform itself, which it has done very slowly and hesitantly so far, it is likely to diminish in numerical size. I do not believe that most Catholics really want a reformed Church; the unreformed Church offers too many securities to be easily given up. I also believe that the Bishops and Pope—who are geniuses at knowing what people really want—will be slow to reform simply because they are intelligent enough to perceive the great possibility of losses. If they do prove themselves willing to reform, even in the face of opposition, the Church will be stronger but smaller. The great question is whether, as time goes on, they will develop the necessary will to reform. That is a very hard question to answer. A reasonable guess is that they will play things very cool—making room, on the one hand, for the heterodox, while, on the other, continuing to provide solace to those unwilling to change. This will be a tricky course to follow, but perhaps from the viewpoint

of the Popes and Bishops to come about the most practical course
they can choose. I myself would prefer radical reform, but I
would predict a long period of muddling around.

## III. DEWART

If *Church* means ecclesiastical institutions, the only prediction
that can be reasonably hazarded is that the Church will change
drastically in the years ahead. I discard the possibility that
the institutional Church will disappear altogether. Like every
other socio-historical, cultural reality, man's faith must be embodied in institutions, and if no institutions exist to give cultural
form to human experience, or if institutions are destroyed, new
institutions are immediately created by man. But I also discard
the possibility that ecclesiastical institutions will remain substantially unaltered. I deduce this not from the fact that conscious efforts to reform and refashion them are being made by
many progressive elements in the Church but, on the contrary,
from the very strength and outrance of the reactionaries, from
the ineffectiveness of the undecided and from the mediocrity of
the passive. If too many ecclesiastical institutions become simply
*irrelevant* to the real life of the community of believers, mere
reform is insufficient. This is happening already. Thus, radical
changes are not likely to come either through revolution or
through evolution of the institutions from within, but through
the marginalization of many (or perhaps most) of the traditional
institutional forms and the creation of novel ones to take their
place.

But the important question concerns not so much the Church
in the narrow sense considered above, but in the wider yet truer
acceptation which refers to the spiritual corporation of professed
Christian believers. In this respect it should be remembered that
what the Church will be like in the future depends strictly upon
what Christians decide today. Now, the prospects which the
present stage of human evolution opens up for the Christian
faith are without a doubt almost unlimited. Christian belief may
yet become the leading cultural force contributing to the con-

scious self-creation of the human world to come in, say, the next thousand years or two. But the Church may also become even more self-involuted and isolated than it has been in its recent past, nursing its grudges, indulging its melancholy hostilities and hoping that time will soon begin to flow in reverse. Or it may, of course, become anything between these two extremes. The point is that whatever it becomes, it will become what *we* make of it.

Precisely because the new forms of the Church will be creatively determined, extrapolation may be of very limited usefulness here. Nevertheless, on the assumption that certain present trends will continue, it may be suggested that the changes which the Church is likely to undergo (say, within a generation or so) could be subsumed under this heading: the diminution of all institutional forms which rest upon a juridical basis and of all rigid structures and, conversely, the growing importance of institutions grounded upon social relations and of those which have flexible structures. Superimposed upon this there may well be a more general trend towards more informal and more numerous structures, but each less influential and powerful than traditionally. It would not be incorrect to refer to these two trends respectively as the socialization and democratization of the Church. Like human culture as a whole, Christianity may in the future become more of a do-it-yourself affair than at any previous time.

## IV. FRANCIS

I think the most honest answer is that I simply do not know. I do not doubt the Church will endure. But this does not mean, of course, that the Church will necessarily become a more powerful influence in the world.

I suppose finally what any man can say in answer to this is really just what he hopes.

I hope the Church will become an ever stronger influence in the world, speaking out on the problems that face mankind, speaking out for peace, for justice.

I hope that Catholics do not become so enamoured of the

world that they forget the source of their commitment. I hope that today's tendency to activism to the neglect of prayer will not continue and that men will come to realize their very action is dependent on the life of prayer.

Some speak of public and group confession and I hope there will be a recognition that as we are called to community we must come as individuals in a state of unity with God. As every man must find himself in relation to others, he first must establish his relationship as an individual with God.

I hope there will be great saints among us, men and women who love God so much the love for God spills out into love and service for all men.

I suppose any one speaking of this has to comment on structures in the Church. I am not concerned so much with structures as I am with men. There is nothing in the structure of the Church that would hinder the work of the Church if the men within these structures were saints. It is in love of God and love of our fellowmen that we will solve our problems far more than it is in mechanical changes in structure.

## V. MATT

Undoubtedly there will be vast and important changes in the externals—i.e., in church structure, administration, canonical disciplines, liturgical rites and ceremonies, etc. Too, according to present signs and portents, there will be, and indeed there already is, widespread apostasy, schism and heresy such as have seldom been seen before, whilst the vaunted "new freedoms" in the church and in the world at large will, unless a miracle of grace takes place, degenerate into a state of such universal chaos and revolution as to require the worst kinds of repression and force to bring it in check again. But whatever comes, insofar as the Church is headed by Him who said, "I am Who am" and "I will be with you even unto the consummation of the world"—thereby indicating His own eternally changeless nature and being, and hence also the eternality of His Church—there will not be and there cannot be any essential change for the Church either now or in the years ahead. In brief, although we may look for many more external transformations in the temporal mode of the Church's existence, there remains as always the supernatural or eternal essence, which was so strikingly summed up by our Lord Himself in the words: "Heaven and earth will pass away, but My word never!"

The time has come, it seems to me, for devoted Christians to be intent far less with exterior changes and concentrate infinitely more on interior renewal and growth in the changeless Spirit and Truth of the omnipotent Lord and Savior and Redeemer King, who is Christ Jesus!

## VI. SHEED

When John became Pope, I had not the vaguest notion of the changes ten years would bring. Why should I think I can foresee even the next ten years? All I can do is jot down some changes I see as possible.

The Pope's decision on Contraception may mean a great falling away: but the evaporation of faith already evident has nothing to do with contraception and unless it is checked the Church may become a very small body indeed. This would mean a simplification of the administrative structure—less centralisation, within each country and within the Church as a whole; discipline easier, more decisions left to individuals, canon lawyers given other duties, the Church having neither the men nor the money for the unremitting vigilance over daily life that she has come to exercise. The lack of money would mean the cutting down of extra-curricular activities—hospitals and schools for instance—with priests released from such not—obviously—priestly activities as the teaching of mathematics to teen-agers. Indeed, if Catholics were reduced to a tiny fraction of the social body, bringing of the faith to unbelievers would have to be seen as a primary work.

Quite apart from any such reduction in numbers, one change seems to be thrusting itself—while Sunday Mass will continue to be in Church, it may become normal for week-day masses to be in private homes (in, say, four years a thousand houses in any one parish could be thus honored, Mass really brought to the people).

Do I see these changes as sure? No, only as **possible**.

Do I want them? Some of them.

# 25. COMMUNISM

## I. Buckley

Communism is changing its forms here and there and it always has. Whether or not it is changing more or less rapidly than Christianity is an open question. I do think that the premises of Communism as understood by Communists are unassimilable by Christianity. I am aware, for instance, of the distinctions that Father Dunne has made between philosophic socialism and programmatic socialism and I think that they are valid distinctions. I think it is perfectly possible to have Christianity and certain communistic—with a small c—forms, but if Communism persists in its devotion to the materialization of the human experience then of course it has got to be rejected.

I don't think you want me to give my opinions on the strategic quarrel we have with Communism and therefore I won't. Suffice it to say that I agree with Father John Courtney Murray in his understanding of Pope John's observation in *Pacem in Terris* that the forms of certain obnoxious ideologies have changed so as to permit a conscientious Catholic to take a different position towards these forms. Father Murray felt that Pope John was referring here to the liberalism which was condemned by Leo XIII rather than to the Communism that was condemned by Pius XI.,

I do envision Communism moving to the right and democracy moving to the left, to the disadvantage of democracy. I do think that the demands of Communism are such as to be incompatible with minimum standards of human freedom, privacy and decency. The politics of convergence, to the extent that they suggest an actual amalgamation, are noxious. To the extent that they simply mean a modus vivendi they are perfectly and utterly and totally desirable. The convergence phenomenon was first called to my attention by Whittaker Chambers twelve years ago. He used a different metaphor—he said something about how two balls of wax will melt into a single tallow. This is what he foresaw, very gloomily, because he was quite persuaded that the principle victim of that amalgamation would be the essential faith of the West. I very definitely see that as happening and I very definitely see it as happening to the disadvantage of the West, and I deeply regret it.

## II. CALLAHAN

So far as possible, Christians should attempt to engage Communists in dialogue. As they do so, however, they should recognize the possibility that this dialogue may go nowhere at all. They should also recognize the possibility that they may be "duped," and that their willingness to enter into dialogue may be used to "lull" them—in short, they should recognize the possibility that much of what the most fanatical anti-communists say about the dangers of dialogue could be true. I emphasize this point, not because I think this is a very real danger, but only because it seems to me a great mistake to try and justify dialogue on a practical basis, i.e., by trying to argue that it will "work," or that it entails no dangers, or that it is justified because Communism is changing or may be able to change. The best motive for dialogue is simply that Christians have the duty of loving their fellow men, even if these men appear in the guise and reality of "the enemy," and that one important way of loving another is to attempt to talk with him. In practice, it seems to me that Communism can and has changed (just as the other partner in the dialogue, Christianity, can and has changed), and thus that dialogue is likely to bear very good practical fruits. But this is a very subordinate reason for dialogue; the main reason, whatever the consequences, is the moral reason.

## III. DEWART

It is significant that Communism has been, as a matter of historical fact, generated wholly from within the Western Christian world, without the slightest adventitious contribution from other cultures. For this reason Communism must be described, culturally speaking, as a Christian phenomenon. To talk about Communism is to talk about *our* Communism: to pretend that Communism is a foreign evil is to misunderstand our own Christian history and to misjudge ourselves overleniently, if not also self-righteously. Hence, the overcoming of Communism makes sense only if it is understood as the overcoming of our own Christian evil and of our own Christian mistakes, mismanagement and misjudgement. Conversely, the redemption of Communism is the recognition of the truth of Communism as a Christian truth betrayed by the Church of Christian believers and kept alive by the Church of Christian unbelievers through schism, heresy and apostasy. Of course, this kind of truth is very difficult to recognize. For its recognition is painful, as always is the recognition of one's own mistakes.

Yet, to a small but surprising extent this has already been done. For example, article 19 of Vatican II's *Constitution on the Church and the Modern World* acknowledges that "believers themselves frequently bear some responsibility" for modern atheism, not simply (as had been previously admitted) in the sense that the *moral* infidelities of believers may have caused scandal, but also because "faith" and "doctrine" themselves may sometimes "conceal rather than reveal the authentic face of God and religion." Perhaps more significant yet is the implicit recognition by the post-conciliar Church of the socio-historical and self-creative nature of man (it is indeed this implicit recognition, as yet only semi-conscious, which is the ferment at work in the post-conciliar Church and which is found disrupting and upsetting). But Christian believers have yet to admit how much remains to be learned from Marxism—and specifically from Marxist and other atheisms, though Arthur Gibson's *The Faith of the Atheist* should move many to an appreciation of the importance and magnitude of the task.

## IV. FRANCIS

It isn't quite fashionable to be anti-Communist these days so rather than commit that modern sin of not being fashionable let me just say I am committed to belief in the inherent worth of every human being.

That doesn't help things much, though, for when I say this I am saying I am anti-Communist and I wind up being just as unfashionable as I would have been had I been more direct.

What is basically the difference between Communists and Christians is their view of man. For me as a Catholic every human being has worth in himself and the society gains its meaning because it is made up of individuals. The Communist thinks the society is important and the individual derives his importance from the fact he is a part of the society.

The two positions are diametrically opposed. There is no need for us to dialogue on the level of our political opinions, our view of economic or social problems. The difference is in our view of man and society.

It isn't just a philosophical argument either. It influences the attitudes on all problems. A Communist government comes into control. It has no qualms about ending freedom of the press, freedom of speech, political opposition. This isn't an accidental position. It comes from the basic view of man and society. Since it is the whole society that is of primary importance, it follows that the rights of individuals are not as important as that of the society. Therefore, it is in the best interests of all that the right of freedom of the press, freedom of speech, freedom of political opposition, be denied to individuals. The Communist government does not hesitate to move ruthlessly against political opponents; again this action stems naturally from the basic philosophy of man.

I'm well aware that Catholics lately have been engaging in debates and dialogues with Communists. That's all right with me, so long as they keep on the subject—which is the basic problem of how you view man and society. From what I read of these encounters, most of them have been off the subject.

I am convinced that Communism itself is a great danger to free men. I know that the popular thing to say today is that we've learned Communism isn't monolithic and we should give up thinking of it as some sort of international bogey-man.

Well, it may be that Yugoslavians and Russians don't get along very well but they both tossed writers who dared to write even in gently critical fashion into the same kind of prisons. Obviously there are political reasons for Chinese and Russian Communists to antagonize each other. But basically they operate from the same political and philosophical basis. Don't make any big bets on the death of the Communist monolith. If the time comes that the free world is forced to fight for its life, don't count on divisions within world Communism.

So I guess I wind up being unfashionably anti-Communist but then it isn't my primary position—just a by-product of my affirmation of the importance of every individual.

## V. Matt

By comparison with the problems beginning to pour in upon the Western World and the all but universal upheaval even within the Church itself, Communism whether in the East or elsewhere, begins to pale, and the central issue, it seems to me, is Atheism in all shades and forms.

## VI. McLuhan

Communism in any practical sense of the word is something that happened over a hundred years ago. It is typical of our inability to look at the present that all utopian writers describe the past that lies immediately behind them. This is as true of Dante whose dream was of the ancient Roman Empire of the past as of Thomas More whose *Utopia* presented a mosaic of the immediate present and of medieval monasticism. The utopia of Don Quixote was, of course, a little more on the comic side, but it, too, was an idealistic attempt to recover the immediate past. With Karl Marx we enter into utopianism of a more formidable kind of hardware and industrialism. He failed to notice that the world that he lived in had already become communist. That is to say, the ordinary working man of his time had access to postal services, highway services, rail services, educational and public services of many kinds, which were far beyond the means of any private wealth to set up or control. I think Communism occurs technically at a time when the service environments provided for the ordinary person are themselves greater than those which the wealthiest person in the community can provide for himself. In our own time, this kind of service environment which is Communism has gone so far beyond any of Marx's dreams that there is no excuse for our talking about the threat of "the rising tide of Communism" unless we are talking about something that is happening inside our own borders and inside our own communities. Our telephone systems, our entertainment systems, our networks which are not practically free services are of such vast expense and cost as to exceed the dreams of all the private wealth in the world. Moreover, no wealthy person could now imagine having access to such services unless they were available simultaneously to the humblest citizen. It is typical of most men's anxieties and panics that they are located in the past and go along with a complete unawareness of the present threats and realities. The present is always a much more terrifying thing than the past and seems to elicit much less attention for that reason. People can feel a little more comfortable in looking back into Bonanza land or into the world of John Wayne's frontier and the Cartwrights. They can feel a little more at home in that kind of rugged world than they do in the immediate present and, therefore, they seem to try to refresh their images of themselves and their communities by this attempt at retrospect while carefully avoiding any contemplation of the present.

## VII. Sheed

What is Communism? We cannot learn what it is by studying Russia or Poland or Jugo-Slavia any more than we can learn what

Christianity is by studying Brazil or the United States. Each country has mingled the original doctrine—of Marx as of Christ —with too much of itself. Marx might well wince every time he hears some piece of savagery attributed to the Communists, as Christ at some of the horrors of the Crusades—named after the Cross on which he died for love of men. The panic fear of Communism with which our air is now laden should be called fear of Russia, fear of China.

Discussion of Communism must begin with what it meant in the mind of Marx; we are discussing it here, I presume, because of the attraction it has for so many Christians, and Marx is their man.

Part of the difficulty in this is that the key to Marx's thinking was that all human needs could be met within the boundaries of this world, this life. His denial of God, of life after death, of any authority in Christ—these negations were not extras, which we can quote or explain away as peripheral, they were basic: we note his fury at any who called themselves Communists while holding on to them. Yet it may well be that to bring in God and immortality and Christ, however much he may have hated the idea, might produce a better monument to him than we have yet seen.

What is left of Marxism when the anti-religious negations are eliminated? He had certain insights—the (elective?) as part of man's definition, for instance, the importance of the economic factor, the necessity of striving here on earth for the most perfect society, the distinction between society and state, the desirability of the state's withering away. In so far as these are of value, is there any point in working for them under the name of Karl Marx? Has the world's experience since his death introduced elements unforeseen by him even unto these? There is no space here for discussion of questions so vast. But that, it seems to me, is what the discussion would have to be about.

# 26. VIETNAM

## I. BUCKLEY

As a Christian I need ask myself whether Vietnam passes the orthdox tests of the just war. In my opinion it does. It does so satisfactorily as to perhaps end us up with a really horrendous dilemma, namely, have we been pursuing our objective with such a scrupulous concern for not doing unnecessary damage to alien property or alien lives, as in fact to find ourselves having prolonged the war and caused more strategic suffering than would have been caused if we had permitted ourselves a clearer military approach to the problems at hand. I feel this is the case; I believe there would have been less suffering and would be more people alive today if in 1965 we had responded conclusively.

The Vietnam war is not only interesting in all the orthodox senses militarily, in terms of colonialism, and in terms of psy-war, but it is interesting also in the sense that it tests the capacity of a democratic country to respond gradually and responsively to provocations more or less pari passu. It may very well be that we will discover, after we meditate the experience of Vietnam, that we should have done something dramatic that would have brought the war quickly to an end. But we may also discover that it is almost impossible to do the dramatic thing in a democracy, and especially in a democracy which encourages dissent from the strategic propositions that made us go to Vietnam in the first instance. In short, we may find out as a result of Vietnam that the proper way to deal with Vietnams in the future is by an almost obliterative reaction, which reaction, however, we may not be permitted by the essential inhibitions of a democracy.

## II. CALLAHAN

The Vietnamese war long ago ceased being a moral war. The United States should immediately withdraw from the war. At the present rate of destruction, there will be nothing left of the country; to talk of democracy and freedom of choice under such circumstances is illusory. The Church's teaching on just war could well and easily be invoked in condemnation of the war; it is a shame that so few Catholics have done so. But then the just war doctrine has never, so far as I know, been invoked during a war, except in defense of the war. It remains another one of those splendid doctrines which have never been allowed to have any practical import.

## III. DEWART

I cannot decide which distresses me more deeply: the bodily injury inflicted by the United States upon Viet Nam, or the spiritual injury inflicted by the United States upon itself by waging war on Viet Nam. And it is especially distressing that American Catholics are in their distinct majority aligned with a war than which a more evidently unjust one is scarcely imaginable. It is a consolation, however, that the American people have not given themselves over to this injustice without an inner crisis of conscience. Paradoxically, American democracy has never been more admirable than at this time, when the emergence of a public American moral conscience, however minoritarian, has done much to blunt some of the guilt of what amounts to a collective act of creeping genocide. Yet, one must also fear for American democracy, which has never been in such grave danger as it is now, when its institutions are subverted at the highest levels of government through doubletalk, misleading propaganda and outright deceit—directed not even at the American government's foreign enemies, but at its own constituents.

One must also grieve, of course, at the hardship, injury and death suffered by Americans in the field. Nevertheless, the least friendly wish one could harbour against the American people would be the wish that they might *win* the Viet Nam war. One hopes against all reasonable hope that the United States will eventually recognize its moral (and not merely its political) mistake. Only the open and frank ackowledgment of a change of heart will regain for it the respect of the world. Of course, before this happens enough Americans must first recognize that their country has taken the wrong path and that its course must be reset. Unfortunately, there are no signs that this will happen very soon—nor that American Catholics, with but the well-known few exceptions, are likely to take an active part in the moral conversion of their own national society.

## IV. FRANCIS

We regret the Buchwalds and the Dachaus after the moment for decision that might have prevented them has passed.

A million refugees fled the totalitarianism of North Vietnam because they believed their freedom would be guaranteed in South Vietnam. Were we to fail our commitment to them then in another generation we would have a new reason to suffer under the guilt of failure.

The Communists, both those from North Vietnam and those left to carry on the revolution in South Vietnam more than a decade ago, have consistently escalated the war against the people living in South Vietnam.

I find it a strange perversion of moral values to speak of the U.S. participation in Vietnam as immoral when it is clear to me that the North Vietnamese and the Viet Cong have consistently carried on a campaign of terrorism designed to bring the whole of Vietnam under the dictatorship of the north.

I despise war. But in an imperfect world, the choice is sometimes between peace and surrender to an aggressor who would destroy all vestiges of freedom. It is this, I believe, that is at stake in Vietnam.

I do not doubt that if we leave Vietnam the aggressors will conquer. Just as they destroyed all who opposed them when they gained control in North Vietnam so they will do the same if they gain control in South Vietnam. The difference this time, however, will be that the refugees will have no place to go.

Our failure to fulfill the commitment in Vietnam will not only affect the neighboring countries, bringing about their eventual downfall, but it will influence the whole free world. We will have demonstrated to all that in a crisis we cannot be counted on and that Communism is the wave of the future.

This will then inevitably lead to a confrontation at some other place in the world and surely bring about the Third World War that all of us want to avoid.

The solution in Vietnam? If the war is justified, as I believe it is, then we must win it in a way that will cost the least in human lives. Because we have carried on an essentially defensive war, allowing the Communists the strategical initiative, we are involved in endless sacrifice of lives. It is only by gaining the strategical initiative that we can prevent a long war of attrition that will destroy South Vietnam and sacrifice the lives of our allies and ourselves.

My only doubt is whether the national will would allow this. The new umbrellas of Munich are so prevalent that public opinion may not allow the necessary steps. If so then we might as well kneel down now and practice the mea culpas we'll be saying as free men who acted too little, too late, in another decade.


## V. MATT

I stand by Pope Paul in this matter. Last January the Pope proclaimed a "day of Peace," underscoring, however, that he was calling for "a true peace," a "just and balanced peace" and not a peace "based on a false rhetoric" of deceit and duplicity designed to "mask sentiments and actions of oppression and party interests." The Pontiff emphasized his hope that no one would be misled by his unflagging concern for world peace. In his words: ". . . it is to be hoped that the exaltation of the idea of peace may not favor the cowardice of those who fear it may be their duty to give their lives for the service of their country and of their own brothers, when these are engaged in the defense of justice and liberty." "Peace," the Pope said, "is not pacifism; it does not mask a base and slothful concept of life, but it proclaims the highest and most universal values of life: truth, justice, freedom, love." His program of peace, the Pontiff suggested, was not to sell out these values, but to preserve and protect them. In fact, he insisted, a peace program worthy of the name must be defended "against the snares of tactical pacifism (which is) designed to smother in men's minds the meaning of justice, of duty, of sacrifice." It is noteworthy that the *N.Y. Times* (Dec 23) headlined its report of the Pope's remarks thus: "Pope Appeals For a Peace Without Victory." The fact is, of course, that he did nothing of the kind. The Pope insists, as the Church always has insisted, on the rightful defense of "the highest and most universal values of life." His explicit condemnation of a false pacifism, which would supinely permit the highest values of life to be jeopardized and even destroyed without lifting a finger, gives the lie to the *Times* headline. In point of fact, even the *Times'* own quotations from the Pontiff's remarks on the subject, categorically disprove the above headline. The Pope, according to the *Times,* "said he was certain that the end to be pursued in Vietnam was not 'victory which oppresses, but security, peace and liberty for all'!" In other words, the Pope, while earnestly pleading for peace, is far from suggesting peace at any price. He is asking for a just and honorable peace, a peace which is neither vengeful nor unduly oppressive. Victory with justice, yes! The sooner the better. But victory without justice, or even a cowardly retreat in the face of an unjust and oppressive enemy, this is not victory! Nor is it Christian!

The Pope's words become more and more pertinent with each passing hour. He has clearly differentiated between the Com-

munists "peace program" and the peace of Christ in the Reign
of Christ. Some of our liberal clergy, please note!

## VI. McLuhan

What could be more poetically complex than the Pueblo
episode? It is like a multi-levelled medieval allegory. The very
name of the ship plays a symbolic role. A group of nonliterates
captured the intelligence center of the greatest and most advanced Power in the world. It is very much a reversal of that
day in 1532 when Francisco Pizarro with 300 cavalry overthrew
the vast Inca empire in three hours. The Pueblo episode is an
outer form of the inner change which is taking place in our
Western world. The Vietnam war is symbolic in its own way.
It is our first TV war, and such is the public participation that
the traditional separation between the military and the civilian
seems to have been eliminated. The first World War had been a
railway war in which vast numbers of troops were deployed
against each other. In Vietnam there is a return to guerilla warfare of a primitive kind exactly in accordance with the de-cen-
tralization of our improved communications. In Vietnam we have
no territorial objectives. It is not a goal but an image that we
seek. We seek the recovery of a lost identity of national purpose
and definition which has been dissolved by our own improving
technologies.

The effort to recover the image of a society dedicated to clearly
defined objectives and goals has no meaning for the younger
TV generation for whom goals, territorial or socialistic, are
equally meaningless. In the Vietnam thing does there lurk
some vague memory of what in the 1920's used to be called the
Yellow Peril? Do we think that by pushing the Westward movement all the way into the East we can free ourselves from this
peril? Is there not far more likelihood that such a push will
merely merge us with the Oriental thing? Are not the sitars and
the gurus of today far more indicative of Western disillusion
than the Mah Jong and the kimonas of the 1920's? Now the
Orient is inside us. In the age of the inner trip outer goals and

objectives lost their meaning in a total all-at-once world of electric circuitry. Is it this panic about the loss of identity that inspires and confuses the Vietnam project?

## VII. SHEED

As a man I have my own reasons for opposition to the war in Vietnam, reasons strongly held but not special to me as a Catholic. I should feel them as strongly if I had long ago left the Church. They do not belong therefore to this book. But the war has raised two questions which affect Catholics particularly. The first is the issue of conscience: whether State commands or Church, it is always wrong to do what one holds to be wrong. One *may* be wrong in so holding it, but one *must* be wrong in doing it.

The second is the demand that the Church—in effect the Pope, or a national hierarchy—should speak out in condemnation of the war. Perhaps it should. But it raises the more general question of the Church's intervention in the affairs of nations. And I should like to glance at that. As a general principle this sort of intervention should be infrequent—it is for the Church to teach us the rules of right and wrong conduct, of sin and virtue, committed to it by Christ, but the instructed Catholic should normally form his own judgment of individual social and political situations according to these rules. The Church is not the Pope and hierarchy—the laity are in it too. And there is a civil sphere which is especially their concern. If their emergence continues *and* their instruction, it will cease to seem normal that their voice should always be uttered by the clergy.

# 27. RIGHT-WING CATHOLICISM

## I. BUCKLEY

I think right-wing Catholicism is confused. However there are aspects of it which I find totally persuasive and highly admirable, most conspicuously a relationship toward the Church which I consider to be the proper relationship. I once got into a great deal of trouble, and it is almost amusing that it was as recently as 1962, for publishing in a secular journal a slightly scandalous jingle "Mater si, Magistra no". It strikes me as incredible that so soon after that sin heard around the world, which even made the pages of the *New York Times*, one finds that the very people who were most censorious at that particular moment would consider it absolutely unnoticeable now.

Right-wing Catholicism has to commend it a continuing acceptance of the relationship between the Church and the laity. I don't mean by this that we desire the kind of servility that would cause us simply to blindly accept whatever hiccup the local bishop uses to instruct us in his particular eccentricity. But I do mean by it that we feel an essential faith that the Church continues to be the repository of a divine mission. The divine mission being to instruct us in the clutch of tangled circumstances in the right thing to do.

Unfortunately there are a lot of accretions around right-wing Catholicism. There is for instance the unfortunate tendency, the ultra-montanist tendency, to understand velleities expressed by this or that Pope in this or that circumstance as perennially bind-

ing. There is a certain amour propre, a desire to think of oneself as sort of superior to other people. All of this I reject. Nevertheless I do believe that the so-called right-wing Catholics are
the likelier successors to those who sweated for the survival of
the word in the catacombs than are the left-wing Catholics.

## II. CALLAHAN

Though I reject just about everything right-wing Catholicism
stands for, I have considerable respect for it. It is not easy to
be a right-wing Catholic these days: most of the younger people,
the press and the theologians oppose them, as does the whole
contemporary culture. It takes a fair degree of conviction and
perseverance to keep going in the face of such powerful ob-
stacles; normally, we would call such people "prophets." Yet
since I do not believe in most of their principles, I am just a bit
reluctant to give them the high title of "prophet"; much of what
right-wing Catholicism stands for seems to me very dangerous.
Nonetheless, I would hope that right-wing Catholicism will try
to exercise a prophetic function. I am quite convinced that much
of what goes under the title of "left-wing Catholicism" is just
as much a selling-out to the culture as its right-wing critics say.
The only trouble is that I am not sure exactly where the selling-
out is taking place. Right-wing Catholicism can, if it is shrewd,
perceptive and sensitive enough, help me to see better the folly,
obvious and latent, in some of my own positions. I am convinced
that the folly is there, mainly because I see no reason to presume
that my own positions, or those who exist in my ideological
branch of the Church are inherently any wiser than the opinions
of those who went before. To the extent that right-wing Catholicism can demonstrate its power to transform the Christian, to
that extent will it provide an effective witness to values the left-
wing is prone to neglect: tradition, order, authority, law. I have
yet to see an effective witness to these values from the right,
but it is perfectly possible that the right-wing will learn how
to give such witness.

## III. DEWART

Everyone has heard about the proverbial father who so deeply, yet so selfishly and myopically, loves his child that he provokes the child's rebellion—and who indeed reacts to the child's rebellion by becoming bitter and self-encapsulated. Mediaeval Christianity successfully fathered a new level of human self-awareness, but was unable to understand the product of its own creativity. Selfish zeal and pride prevented the Church from rising to the challenge presented to it by its own creature; it became gradually isolated from human experience, increasingly self-involuted and ever more exclusively concerned with the preservation of its past and the enjoyment of its happy memories. As is well-known, Pope John suggested that this attitude should be re-examined. In that suggestion consisted his greatness—and on that issue the Church has become divided.

For the current division of the Church is at its most basic level a conflict between two opposite attitudes towards temporality. The conservatism or traditionalism which matters (for it is, as I see it, injurious to the Church) is not necessarily that which is connected with any given doctrine: neither the age nor the lack of vogue of any opinion is a reliable indication of its adequacy. The traditionalism that matters, and which the Gospel condemns, is that which stems from fear of the future, and which adheres to specific traditional doctrines because of the belief that if the deposit of faith is kept intact, so that it may be unearthed at the end of history and returned to God, the Church will be able to claim the reward of a faithful steward.

I wish to stress that no given theological position as such spells conservatism in this sense. And I take it as axiomatic that for honest opinions honestly held, whether liberal or conservative, no one should have but respect and open mind. What is neither admirable nor admissible is the attitude of so many Catholics at all levels of the Church who appear to think that *No* is always a safe answer—and indeed that safety is always convertible with prudence, and that prudence can always be shown by abdicating one's conscience when one cannot make up one's own mind.

## IV. FRANCIS

I suppose what is needed here is a definition. It is to be assumed that we're not talking about the political views of Catholics. But I'd be hard put to define exactly what a Right Wing or a Left Wing Catholic would be.

Therefore, I'll choose to talk about that group of Catholics today who call themselves Traditionalists.

Their primary objection is to the new liturgy, although this does not cover all of their objections.

More than two decades ago, I joined the Vernacular Society because I believed that the liturgy in the language of the people would be more meaningful. This I considered my right and, believing as I did, my duty.

But with the Mass in Latin I participated as fully as possible. When Pope Pius XII called for active participation, using the Latin responses, I did this. Today I participate even more fully in the new liturgy and I am happy about it.

But just as I thought it permissible for Catholics to advocate the vernacular so do I think it permissible for Catholics who believe this way to advocate for a return to the Latin. I believe they are wrong but I support completely their right.

The exception I take is to those who refuse to participate in the liturgy as it is at this moment; some have even sought to disrupt the liturgy. This attitude isn't unique. When Pius XII called for participation in the Latin Mass, there were some vernacularists who stood aside because they thought it a compromise that might harm the chances for what they sought.

The new liturgy will some day be the old liturgy; certainly we should not immobilize our means of worshipping God. But the liturgy that is most important to me is the liturgy that I share at this particular moment in history with the rest of the People of God.

If by Right Wing Catholicism is meant that small minority who might stand aside as petulant children refusing to worship God with their brothers because they don't like the new liturgy then I think this is wrong.

## V. MATT

I abhor both terms. I am a *Roman Catholic,* period!

## VI. SHEED

I don't like labelled Catholicism; labels tend to harden into parties, and parties into enmities. At their extremes the two "wings" are like two sects, not serving therefore the work Christ founded his Church to do—to carry his gifts of truth and life to all nations. It is excellent that Catholics should use their own minds on the development of the Church's teaching and the renewal of the Church's structure: but only if they can differ without hatred, if they can extend their ecumenism to embrace their co-religionists.

# 28. LEFT-WING CATHOLICISM

## I. BUCKLEY

Left-wing Catholics are highly idealistic, highly desirous of extending the  influence of the Church. But I honestly think that they feel their primary responsibility is to adapt the Church to the world rather than vice versa. We see them saying in effect to the world, "Look, the Catholic Church really doesn't amount to much more than a sort of helpful, interesting and even pleasant congeries of symbols and attitudes, and if you just hang on awhile we will tame the Church so that it won't really inconvenience you in your passage through this vale of tears."

They are doing a great strategic disservice; they are attacking the unique strength of the Church which is the strength to say "all the world is wrong for no better reason than that it disagrees with us—we being the Church—and it doesn't matter at all if Mr. Gallup yields a result that is 99.9% against us, the fact of the matter is that we are right and they are wrong." This, I think, is the strength of the Church, not merely because there are some of us left that still have faith in the warrant that the gates of hell will not prevail against the Church but also because we disbelieve that the world is necessarily progressing in the direction of sanctimony and what Professor Vogelin calls the "immanentization of the eschaton," something which we anti-Utopians want to resist. I do think that the left-wing of the Catholic Church tends to be arguing in that direction.

174

## II. Callahan

In response to this category, I would like to state my own general stance toward my own positions throughout this book. As the range of my responses indicates, I probably belong in the left-wing camp. For some years now that has been my spiritual home, my source of Christian formation and education, my primary circle of friends and colleagues. To left-wing Catholicism, I owe just about everything I am as a Christian. But this does not mean that I am totally satisfied with it. The main thing it has given me is the psychological freedom and the theological encouragement to be speculative and playful. That is just what I have tried to be in my responses throughout this book. Please don't be misled by the frequently dogmatic tone; the required short responses account for much of it. Just about everything I have said here represents what I happened to think at the moment I wrote it. A year ago, I would have given some very different answers; a year from now I am likely to be appalled at some of the answers here. I could have great fun even now refuting all my responses; and it would be very easy. But left-wing Catholicism has taught me not to worry very much about such shifts; for that I am grateful, even if such vacillation may disturb my readers—and sometimes (in fact) it disturbs *me*.

But I am also dissatisfied with much left-wing Catholicism. Socially and institutionally it seems to me to have made a much greater contribution than it has intellectually. Increasingly, left-wing Catholicism is prone to drift off into an intellectual obscurantism and rhetorical vacuity. To replace the old theological castles, it is building new, up-to-date theological dream houses; most of them seem to me flimsy and highly flammable. My own stress on a bodily God is a way of countering the evanescent new Gods being proposed by left-wing Catholicism: the God-of-process; the eschatological God; the God of mystery beyond mystery; the God of history. Moreover, I think there is a very real danger in the way left-wing Catholicism has become so respectable among secular intellectuals. I am writing this at a very nice desk, in a very nice house, and most of the money for these

amenities has come from the unsought but profitable business of
being known as a left-wing, OK Catholic, one who can be counted
on to knock the same things in the Church that most enlightened
secular minds have always knocked. "Why don't you get ————
to write the article for you?"—I once suggested to the editor
of a major secular magazine who wanted an article on celibacy.
When I told the editor that the person I had in mind was an
intelligent conservative, one who had some sensible arguments
for obligatory celibacy, I was told "Oh no, we want a Catholic
like *you*, because we know you're against required celibacy."
Since it is true that I oppose required celibacy, I was their man.
I can't say I felt happy about the whole conversation; in a very
subtle way, I think I was being had. I suspect that many of us
left-wing Catholics are being had these days, and I worry about
that. The game of being more-radical-than-thou is a big one in
left-wing Catholicism. The coincidence between this radicalism
and upper-level main-line secular American intellectual values is
worthy of continual suspicion. On the whole, I don't think I will
be happy with left-wing Catholicism until it has learned how to
be prophetic to the upper-strata of American secular liberalism;
at present, we are just trailing along behind, happy to provide it
our theological blessing. It is not hard at all to be prophetic in the
face of conservative Christianity; or in the face of a status quo
racist, war-mongering society; or in the face of bureaucratic
bishops. But it is extraordinarily hard to be prophetic to hippies,
New Leftists, and those who are already with-it to an extraordinary degree. That seems to me the real challenge now to left-
wing Catholicism.

## III. DEWART

The truth that novelty does not necessarily mean improvement
is so obvious it is scarcely worth stating. It may be more important
to recall that the Christian Church is built upon a faith that hopes
in love—a faith that of its very nature culminates in man's present
self-disposition *for the sake of what is yet to come.* In this context,
conservatism is a thoroughly and unambiguously unchristian posture, and a progressive attitude is the only one which the Christian

faith can genuinely inspire. There are, of course, illegitimate forms of liberalism and progressivism, and it is not always easy to distinguish them from the legitimate. But the following principles may help.

The human future is created in the present—it does not come about through the mere passage of time. But the present is the outcome of the past. Hence, the future can be created, in the last analysis, only out of the past. To presume to cut oneself off from the past in order to fashion the future is to attempt an impossibility —the achievement of which is of the essence of sin. On the other hand, it would be unreasonable to imagine that the Kingdom of God could be constructed without mistakes, without delays and without temporary failures. If, despite the possibility of error on either extreme, the Christian must ultimately favour progressivism, the reason is that for the Christian it should be better to fail after having made his attempt, than never to have tried at all.

## IV. FRANCIS

Again I seek a definition. I would assume, again, that we are not speaking of political positions.

If left-wing Catholicism can be interpreted as being seen in the positions of those who do not accept the magisterium of the Church, who would oppose those positions enunciated by the Pope, who would refuse to accept the role of the episcopacy in the governing of the liturgical forms, then I would believe it destructive of the meaning of community.

I am well aware that there is a role for speculative theology, that prophetic voices should be heard in the Church, but even speculative theology must be governed by some boundaries of commitment to theological truths and not all voices that claim to be prophetic are the voices of true prophets.

## V. MATT and

## VI. SHEED

Cf. Right-Wing Catholicism.

# 29. WHAT I WOULD DO IF I WERE POPE

## I. BUCKLEY

Obviously what I would do if I were Pope is simply pray. I don't doubt of course that the Pope does pray, but I do think that the Pope needs to know that there are Catholics in the world who deeply cherish the Church and him and the institution and that we will stay with him. And if his conscience leads him in the direction of a new militancy, however divisive it might appear to him, he will find a gladdening number of people who are prepared to go with him to the brink and stay with him because we do believe that the desacralization of the Church is manifestly not to its advantage. I think it's probably an improper question to ask "what would you do if you were Pope." If you were Pope or I were Pope, it would only be because we were tapped by the Holy Ghost and if we were tapped by the Holy Ghost, like Joan of Arc, it would only be because our mission was manifest. But the disclosure of that mission presumably would be a part of the process of investiture, and we would know immediately what it was that we were tapped to do.

## II. CALLAHAN

If I were Pope, I would probably present a rather ambiguous image. For I would, on the one hand, try to be very radical and active institutionally, socially and politically; but, on the other, try to be moderate and conciliatory theologically. Institutionally,

178

I would take prompt steps to bring about full collegiality in the Church, at all levels. I would do away with the College of Cardinals, disband most of the Roman congregations—or turn them into purely advisory bodies—take steps to turn over the Vatican wealth to worthwhile causes, sell the Vatican art to the museums of the world and, in general, strip the Holy See of all its worldly resources and props. I would ask (not order) all of the bishops of the world to take similar steps with the valuables of their dioceses. I would further ask all of the bishops and pastors of the world to cease building churches, and instead to concentrate their financial resources on the alleviation of poverty and misery. I would also try to address myself more specifically to the problems of the world than the Popes have traditionally done. Theologically, though, I would act in a more moderate way. While I would not condemn someone who held views like mine (in these responses), neither would I go out of my way to commend them. Instead, I would ask all parties in the theological disputes today to preserve the tradition of rationality in the Church, ask them to take account of the history of the Church and encourage them to act toward each other in a sensitive and conciliatory way. I would, in a word, try to be a source of unity and mediation, resisting the temptation to sharply score one or another group, or throw my support to one or another faction. The last thing I would do would be to cast myself in the role of final judge of theological disputes. In general, whether institutionally or theologically, I would encourage everyone to be bold, willing to risk much for the sake of love and truth. I would try to make it clear that the Church must go the whole human route. To be a light to the world, it must have an active mind and body; it must cease trying to save and protect itself, turning its attention and energy instead to liberating and giving itself—and the absolutely necessary first step would be to make itself materially poor as an institution. Finally, if I were Pope I would make a serious attempt to change my own style, which now tends to be too cool, too intellectual, too detached, too bourgeois. Since I might have trouble doing this, though, I think I would soon abdicate, announcing that while I was, hopefully, of some use to the Church, I am not fit to be Pope.

## III. DEWART

It would be easy to interpret this question as an invitation to criticize the incumbent Pope. This is a task which should in no event be undertaken unthinkingly or irresponsibly, but least of all with the presumption which would be implied by any attempt to evaluate the Pope's actual record against the ideal and flawless standard of one's own imaginary performance. I shall not therefore discuss what the Pope should do that he may not be already doing, or that he may not be doing well. I shall discuss instead what I consider to be the desirable characteristics of papal decisions in the light of the needs of the Church at this precise moment of history.

Under contemporary conditions the adequacy of papal teaching depends much less upon content than on form. I have repeatedly made clear in previous sections that in my opinion the Church should consciously undertake the creation of all the novel cultural forms which Christianity must adopt now for the sake of the future of belief—and so it should not surprise the reader if I expressed the hope that papal policies in our time should lead to the self-transformation of the Church into a more truly Universal community. Yet I would not hesitate to say, at the same time, that the best Pope for the Church today is not necessarily a progressive Pope, or that even a highly conservative Pope can contribute immeasurably to the health of the Church. For what matters is not so much whether papal decisions and teachings are progressive or conservative, but whether the Pope speaks and acts with perceptiveness, common sense, candidness, realism and a sense of history—or whether he remains true to the type which has been set in modern times, according to which personal rather than political virtue defines the ideal Pope.

If the opposite is true, the reason is that there is an important difference between what the Church does and what the Pope does, between the direction in which the Church moves and the direction in which the Pope believes it should move—just as there is an important difference between what the Pope intends to achieve and the effect his official acts may actually have upon the history of the Church. It matters little, for instance, whether contemporary Popes are personally humble, if at the same time they have an inflated idea of the power and authority of their office, or whether they are mild and diffident, if their encyclicals project a spiritually overbearing image. The Pope's influence is greater, and his prestige higher, with believer and non-believer alike, with dissident faithful and with unquestioning follower both, when neither his manner nor his speech, neither his behaviour nor his policies, neither his pronouncements nor his teachings, hang heavy with the assumption that if he makes a mistake he has compromised God.

The same idea could be translated to other spheres. Like personal humility, every other virtue is, without a doubt, always a great asset in the discharge of any office. But perhaps we have too long been mesmerized by the memory of the Borgias, overcompensating with the thought that a saintly Pontiff is necessarily a wise Pope. No one proposes that lechery, nepotism and greed should be overlooked. On the other hand, neither a wholesome board nor an innocent handshake, neither chastity nor poverty, neither prayer nor devotion, substitute for good sense, or for timing, or for a feeling with and for what is happening in the world. These are more valuable to any community, as characteristics of its leaders, than any amount of good will and holiness. Sound statesmanship and inspiring government are more important than paternal dutifulness—which may be touching but which is not necessarily effective or relevant to our time.

Thus today's Pope might well not think of himself as commanding (however benevolently) a flock of sheep (however intelligent), but as guiding men who, for all their moral and intellectual shortcomings, can fulfill their Christian vocations only to the degree that they themselves grow in consciousness, creativity and responsibility. The Church today needs the kind of papacy that would be distinguished not so much for its holy fatherhood as for its competent and realistic leadership.

## IV. FRANCIS

I don't really think like this. I am not pope, I will not be pope and so the question is not relevant for me.

But what I pray for always is that the Pope will be a man very close to God, that he will pray even more than he acts, that he will take each action of his public life only after prayer and with great compassion for all men.

I would hope he would be above political considerations, material considerations, and yet in every way concerned for all of mankind. I would hope he would always have an awe-ful realization of the responsibility placed on him and that nothing he would ever say or do would be said or done without this realization.

I hope he will never be influenced only by public opinion, only by what seems pragmatically necessary; I hope he will never seek to appear wise but that if he believes it to be necessary, that he might be willing to seem as a fool in the world.

I hope—and do not doubt that he will—that he will always be faithful to the responsibility of continuing to proclaim to the world the message of Christ and always faithful to that faith that has come through the centuries.

## V. Matt

In the face of current upheaval in the Church and Society I don't know that anyone could do more than the present Pope. A new Syllabus of Errors might be helpful, though I suspect that certain elements in and out of the Church might resort to open violence if such a Syllabus were issued. In any case, I'm afraid the so-called intellectuals in our day—i.e., the Teilhardian evolutionists, materialists, modernists—would ignore it and go their merry way, even as they did when Pius IX and Pius X tried to stop them. In the circumstances perhaps the time has come for the Holy Father, instead of trying to reason with them and contend against them, to ignore them and concentrate on the "little people" among God's People. He made a start in that direction when he went to Fatima last May. He said at the time that he went there in quest of peace—peace for God's People, peace for the Church, and peace for the world. He told us the place to begin to turn back the tide of modern-day anarchy and open revolt: "Have recourse to her," he said, "who for the safety of this world of ours has shown her sweet, luminous and motherly face" to the little children at Fatima. More specifically, the Pope urged prayer and penance as "the sovereign remedies"—Pope Paul's own words!—for the world's present ills. This, of course, is the Fatima message, the message of Mary, Christ's message, and also the Pope's message! They are all agreed! Pope Paul spoke also of the Second Vatican Council when he was at Fatima. He said the Council was nothing if it was not a call to all Catholics and Christians for "a greater awareness, a more intimate collaboration, a more fraternal apostolate" in the divine mission of redeeming and sanctifying the souls of men. But he warned, as he has warned so often, that the Council was not intended to provoke what he called "arbitrary interpretations not authorized by the teaching of the Church." It is not to be construed as giving anyone—whether priests or laity —the right to "disrupt" the Church's traditional and constitutional structure, or to "replace the theology of the true and great Fathers of the Church with new and peculiar ideologies," or to "strip the norms of the Faith" of their vital elements. "We want to ask of Mary," the Pope said, a *living* Church, a *true* Church, a *united* Church, a *holy* Church!"

The question arises: Why, if prayer and penance are "the sovereign remedies" for all of the ills facing the Church and Society in our day—why then does not the Church resume her ancient legislation and prescribe more stringent forms of prayer and penance, instead of permitting these things to be minimized more and more? And if Mary, the Mother of the Church, prescribes prayer and penance—as she did at Lourdes and Fatima—why then does not the Church insist on greater attention and devotion to Mary and her messages, rather than permit her priests and Religious to downgrade these things as "non-liturgical" if not out of style and "anachronistic"?

A few weeks ago the newspapers reported that Pope Paul, while addressing a group of people in the Vatican, suddenly broke down and wept over the disobedience of "sons within the Church." Indeed, he has much to weep about, when dissension and discord and so-called "holy disobedience" have become the order of the day, when Bishops oppose Bishops, priests oppose priests, and the generality of the faithful seem not to have anything more in mind than did the shouting, quarreling, rioting mobs in the days of the bloody French Revolution, when they sang their ribald hymns to Liberty, Equality, and Fraternity—and "Down with the King, down with the Pope, down with sacred traditions and divinely established authority, down with Christ, crucify Him! We want no god but Caesar!"

In the circumstances, it is plain to be seen that Soviet Russia is not the only threat to the world in our day. Bloody persecution and martyrdom beyond description exist there, it is true. But elsewhere in the world today, including in the Universal Church of Christ, we begin to see evidence of kindred things. Let's face it— even a dry martyrdom has begun, a martyrdom more incredible than all the rest, inasmuch as it is directed all too consistently *by* Catholics *against* Catholics—*even against the Pope!* Little wonder the Pope should weep! Shouldn't we all? I recall the reported vision of little Jacinta at Fatima. One very hot afternoon, according to Wm. Thomas Walsh's book, *Our Lady of Fatima,* when even the little children were almost asleep, Jacinta suddenly was heard to exclaim: "Do you not see the Holy Father?" Her companions said no, they couldn't see him. Whereupon Jacinta declared: "I don't know how it is, but I see the Holy Father, in a very large room on his knees, and with his hands over his face, crying. And in front of the house are many people, and some of them are throwing stones at him, others are cursing him and saying foul things to him. Poor little Holy Father! We must pray a lot for him."

I believe Jacinta's prediction is being fulfilled in our day, and also the predictions of Fatima. And is not the Pope's repeated display of anguish a portent perhaps of worse to come. Our Lady said that the Church—meaning all of us—and the Holy Father, would have much to suffer. And indeed, we *are* suffering, even now, are we not, and the Pope is suffering, even as Our Lady said he would. In fact, whether we want it or not, we seem to have replaced fish on Fridays not with the solid meat of greater Christian commitment and dedicated apostolate, but rather we have imposed upon ourselves a far greater penance, a veritable hell on earth, which neither the words of Christ nor Pope nor priest alone can cure but only people in the aggregate, who *cooperate with grace* and *live Christ* as He wills it! Unless and until the People of God determine to do that, by a firm commitment of mind and heart and will, God Himself will never force them or vitiate their freedom, or, let us say, their "right," to go to hell!

## VI. SHEED

I would make it a condition of my resignation that my successor should give an intensity of consideration the Church has not always given to people who really do believe in God and love Him, yet find themselves caught in disobedience to His law which they feel it beyond their power to cope with. Sins of confusion in the mind or want of strength in the will are not the same as sins of rebellion.

# APPENDIX A: HOW FAR DO CONTRIBUTORS REPRESENT VIEWS OF THE CATHOLIC PUBLIC?

To obtain a rough idea of how the attitudes of Catholics in general correspond to the views expressed by the contributors to this book an anonymous survey was taken in May, 1968, among students at a large Catholic university. The student answers were processed by computer. The students included in the tabulated results below are all Catholics. They are college freshmen, about 60% boys and 40% girls. The views are slightly higher in orthodoxy than if upper classmen had been included. The sample was made up of 114 freshmen, from several classes taught by different professors. The following data will offer points of comparison with the beliefs of the contributors.

| Statement | Percent who agree |
|---|---|
| I am firmly convinced that contraception is wrong (before Pope's encyclical) | 20% |
| I believe that Satan exists | 52 |
| I am firmly convinced that the Pope is infallible as defined by the Church | 53 |
| I am firmly convinced that sexual intercourse outside marriage is wrong | 57 |
| I am firmly convinced that there is a hell and that some people go there | 63 |
| I believe in the Virgin Birth of Jesus Christ as taught by the Catholic Church: Mary was a virgin before, during and after Jesus' birth | 74 |

I am firmly convinced that Christ is God                    83
I am firmly convinced that racial discrimination is
    wrong                                                   85

Other data in the survey show that those who follow traditional Church teaching on contraception will overwhelmingly accept the other orthodox statements in the list. The statements lower in the list seemed easier to accept, and those who endorsed a statement will in the great majority of cases also endorse those statements below it. This seems to offer possibilities for classification into four groups, following in part the nomenclature used in the Glock-Stark survey: high orthodoxy, upper medium orthodoxy, lower medium orthodoxy, and low orthodoxy.

In the high orthodoxy group would be those who accept all the statements, including the one on contraception. In the upper medium group are those who accept all the traditional positions mentioned except that on contraception. In the low medium group are those who reject papal infallibility, but do accept the Virgin Birth of Christ (the same group would be very likely to consider Satan merely a symbolic figure and to feel that pre-marital sex may sometimes be justified). In the low orthodoxy group are those who do not accept the doctrine of the Virgin Birth nor the statements above it in the list. In this survey of college freshmen about one fifth are in the high orthodoxy group, about one third in the upper medium, one quarter in the lower medium and one quarter in the low orthodoxy group. Such grouping is a rough approximation and is subject to much qualification. Some may criticize the term "low orthodoxy" as putting that group in a bad light. Others might criticize from an exactly contradictory point of view: convinced that the term "orthodoxy" has a pejorative connotation they would assert that the appellation "high orthodoxy" puts that group in a bad light. If the reader wishes to try to fit the contributors to this book into these categories, that is the reader's privilege.

The results of this survey agree basically (on those points where comparison can be made) with the Glock-Stark study of church members in the San Francisco Bay area, with the Andrew

Greeley report, and with the Gallup poll done for the *Catholic Digest*. When adjustments are made for the different age groups surveyed and for the recentness of the survey, agreement is very close. Comparison with the Manhattan College survey is difficult because of large differences in phrasing of questions.

# APPENDIX B:   TREND AWAY
# FROM ORTHODOXY

Figures no. 1 and no. 2 on the following page show a decline in orthodoxy, comparing each year's class of freshmen. The decline is gradual until 1968, when there is a sharp drop. The sample used is reasonably representative, made up of students from different professors and different campuses. Very possibly the drop in orthodoxy on doctrinal points, accompanied by a jump in orthodoxy on racial discrimination, indicates the result of a new approach to teaching religion in Catholic grammar and high schools. The new approach emphasizes social values more and doctrine less.

One interesting sidelight is that the figures lend no support to the concept of "sex explosion" that one reads so much about. The percentage of those who claimed to have had extra-marital sexual intercourse in the preceding year shows a slight decrease (from 13% down to 9%) over the four year period.

The percentage of students who are convinced that contraception is wrong has plummeted from 52% in 1963-64 to 20% in 1968. Acceptance of papal infallibility has been similarly hard hit: down from 83% to 53%. Belief in hell is down sharply; Sunday Mass attendance and belief that Christ is God have dropped slightly. On the other hand conviction that racial discrimination is wrong has risen from a steady 74% to 85%.

The trends seem to indicate that Catholic teachings which are reinforced by values of secular society are increasingly accepted by the Catholic public; those teaching which are shared by traditional Protestant belief but not by secular society are declining somewhat in acceptance; those teachings which are uniquely Catholic are declining sharply in acceptance by the Catholic public.

190

## Survey of Attitudes of Catholic Freshman Students

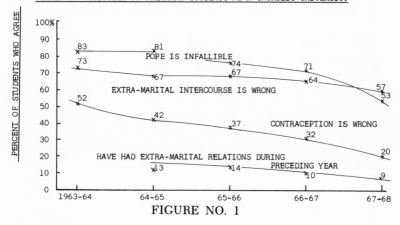

SURVEY OF ATTITUDES OF FRESHMAN STUDENTS AT A CATHOLIC UNIVERSITY

FIGURE NO. 1

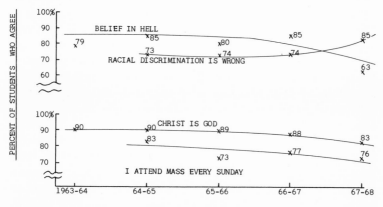

FIGURE NO. 2

Sample size: 1963-4, 154 students. 64-65, 270. 65-66, 150. 66-67, 184. 67-68, 114. The students in the 1963-4 group were upper classmen as well as freshmen. Figures for freshmen would be slightly higher.